SUMMER EXPLOSION

MAST PUBLICATIONS

First published in Great Britian 1994 by

Mast Publications, 31 Beaufort Gardens,
Knightsbridge, London SW3 1QH

This anthology copyright Mast Publications 1994

Copyright of included work remains the property of the author.

Summer Explosion

Edited by
Steve James

All rights reserved. No part of this book may be reproduced or transmitted in any form by any means, electric or mechanical, including photocopying, recording or by an information storage and retrieval system, without permission in writing from the publishers.

ISBN 1-898322-06-6

Published, typeset and distributed by
Mast Publications

Printed and bound by
Input Typesetting Ltd, Wimbledon, London SW19 8DR

Summer Explosion

Summer Madness
Barnaby Welch

"Read all about it,
London's alive",
The streets no longer depress.

The earth has revolved,
Just a little bit closer,
And Mankind starts to undress.

Oh hail the Sun!
King of all stars,
We worship your warm golden rays,

We lie in your light,
Our eyes shut to shield us,
The memory of winter ablaze.

Just blink your eyes once,
And summer is gone,
Before anyone can behold her.

Blink your eyes twice,
And the evil Jack Frost,
Is looking over your shoulder.

∎

Rose Garden
Jo Hodgkins

Raindrops drip from the fingers of the tree,
The grey clouds press down on a writhing sea.
Scurrying cars swish past in the rain
Flotsam gathers at the gurgling drain.
In the garden the satin jewels shine.
Pearls of light gather on petals, fine.
The scent is warm, heady, sublime.
Like a black velvet night in a warmer clime.

Summer Explosion

A Summers Day
D Palmer

The wind it rushes through the grass
A carpet of green as we pass
Natures lawn how it should be
Washed clean with dew for you and me
Country flowers bright with bloom
Pour fragrance fresh this afternoon
And insects buzz idly by
Shining bright in Summer sky.

A butterfly with peacock wings
Flutters by as skylark sings
A scented scene of many a hue
Reds rustic greens and skybright blue
Everything moves in the breeze
Hear the words of rustling trees
And listen for the creatures talking
Hidden but there as we go walking.

For all around is Natures way
A thing of beauty A Summers day.

∎

New Forest In Summer
Violet May Brackstone

Wake up my friend, Wake up,
Hear the distant drums,
Heralding dawns chorus,
Summer has begun.

Entering the forest,
Caravans in tow,
Pitches are designated,
As a temporary home.

Summer Explosion

The tradition of the forest,
Bring us back a thousand years,
Wandering free, ponies
Cattle, squirrels and deer.

Tall pine trees in the forest,
Directed to the sun,
Bringing the smell of essence,
To everyone.

Gorse seed pods are popping,
Flung wild amongst the Ling,
Harebells ringing softly as the
Breezes sing.

Summer spells of the forest,
Lingers on past winter time,
To feel again the pleasure,
In ancient times.

■

Youthful Summer
Mathew Boyde

By the canal, in the fine weather
When I was young, the world was better,
Watery stillness with small ripples
A sunny breeze blows them along
Young companions, easy and carefree
Where are they, now they are mature
We talked of football, and of freedom
Young girls, what we could do to them
Everything clear as politics divide
We knew labour was on our side
The certainty of youth, when I was younger.

We swam in the water, in the best part,
Theory's experts now would shudder,
They know what is best for all,

Summer Explosion

Their minds slowly shrink so small,
On the bank we'd light a fire,
Though the sun's still more than warm
A few cigarettes, we lit after,
Smoking then, was still the norm.
We did not know, how wonderful the world was,
And how it would change, to the one we now have.

■

Bright Days
Olive M Clark

Beautiful blue up in the sky
Cottonwool clouds drifting by
Beautiful flowers to be seen
A touch of grass to set the scene
A walk in the wood is sheer pleasure
To be taken at your leisure
Birds are singing in the trees
Listen to them at your ease
Squirrels scamper, badgers dig
One feels like doing a jig
After gloomy winter days
The sun warms us with its rays
Enjoying the delights of summer
The countryside is such a wonder
Children are playing in the park
Can stay and play until it's dark
I wish I was a child again
To walk again that sunny lane
Cattle lowing in the field
The grass they eat gives out good yield
These lazy, lazy days
Can be enjoyed in different ways

■

Summer's Inspiration
Sue Bevin

With bucket and spade, I built my young dream
and nothing in the world could destroy it.
Solid sand the firm foundation, ice-cream
cone, the castle lanterns, lovingly lit.

With bucket and spade, I built my dream home
and nothing in the world could destroy it.
Though thousands of feet on the beach would roam
my fortress shone safe, dug deep in its pit.

With bucket and spade, creation was born
and nothing in the world can destroy it.
Though Winter's months mark me battered and worn
Summer's Inspiration shall be my wit.

■

An English Country Garden
Brenda E Penney

Shall I water?
Maybe not.
The forecast's simple -
'Fine and hot'.

But what if
Come the early dawn
I wake up
To a thunderstorm?

Suppose they're right
And all the rain
Falls mainly on
That plain in Spain?

But I'm not sure,
And while I dither

Summer Explosion

My busy lizzies
Might just wither.

That clematis
Looks none too bright -
My fuchsias
Are a sorry sight.

No time to waste,
I have a plan -
I'll just ignore
That hose-pipe ban!

∎

Summer Time
Sylvia Armer

The beauty of the summer air
With fragrant flowers everywhere
The trees are decked with leaves of green
Once more the earth in splendour seen

The sky so blue, no hurried cloud
The bird in song that sings out loud
So warm the sun, in sweet delight
It bathes the earth in life and light

Our spirits lift as if on wings
To witness all these lovely things
A humming bee a bird in flight
Sweet scented stocks that fill the night

The stars seen clear on the darkness of sky
Like jewels on a bed of black velvet they lie
Walking in the refreshing rain
I'm glad that summer is here again.

∎

Sunday Menu
Marguerite Walker

Gone to ground,
Husband and hound,
Are in the potting shed.

Away from the kitchen fray.
The whirring mixer,
Clattering dishes.
Cleaning the veges,
Preparation,
Transformation into naked new potatoes.
Pink prawns and green lettuce,
Cucumber wedges.
Roasting aromas.
Apple pie and custard.
Oh! Where is that mustard?
Hum of the microwave,
Quick! Stir the gravy.
Must warm up that pastry.
Please press that knob,
Plates on the hob.
What a relief, gone is the steam.

Dinner is ready,
Paramount to keep steady.
The places are set,
With glasses for wine.
Are periwinkle blue flowers,
Twine by arrangement, amongst the cutlery.
It all looks so fine,
As we gather for grace,
Each one in his place,
Together again. AMEN.

∎

Summer Explosion

It's A Car's Life
Robert Simpson

Car's prepared for the extra load
Waiting to take them on the road
Tyre pressures checked before the trip
Ensuring they'll keep a solid grip

Engine's tuned for the added strain
The longest journey is here again
Toys and bears join the merry horde
Adults and children climb aboard

Summer is here and it's holiday time
Lots of roads and hills to climb
Windows are shining and mirrors gleam
Ready to fulfill the annual dream

Doors keep the passengers safe inside
Ready to go on the long, smooth ride
As the engine roars and the gears grind
Headlights search for peace of mind

Journey's begun in the searing heat
Carpets absorb tired, restless feet
Oil and water try to keep cool
Tending to fail as a general rule

Waiting for a break to get some rest
Being put to the ultimate test
There is no haste to reach the end
Car is seen as a long lost friend

Journey's end is now in sight
Sun-roof lets in air and light
Exhausted and in need of rest
Faithful car has done his best

Parked for the night and safe inside
Feeling smug and full of pride

Life's Summer
Betty Jervis

Let the summer of your life
Burst forth hard on the heels
Of spring, when all was fresh
And new and every special thing
Was tried and tested to define
Its' worth to you.

Now is full summer here to
Prove how youthful exploits
Have removed your fears and
The richly embroidered pattern
Of your early years will display
The worth of you.

Ensure that joy and love take
Pride of place, and cushion
Your sorrows with bright courage
For autumn strides apace, give thanks
For summer's abundant glory - its'
Worth is reflected in you.

∎

Paradox '94
Alexander Southgate

Under a leafy tree, in a dappled glen,
I dream the dreams of summer.
The birdsong a sleepy serenade,
the wind a phantom drummer.

I soar to far off lands.
On the Pegasus' back I fly.
Trapped in ancient Greek mythology,
looking through the Cyclops eye.

Summer Explosion

Shielded from the Gorgon's gaze,
looking toward the sun.
Inside Icarus I now belong,
along time lines I do run.

Gone this land of legends.
Back to reality.
It seemed too vivid to be a dream,
perhaps just an abnormality.

■

The Empire Hotel, Blackpool
Margaret Lewis

The Empire is a happy place,
The staff are full of fun,
The guests all have a smile of their face
From dawn 'til day is done.

There's Thelma with her winning ways,
And Darren with his charm,
So, all our days are happy days,
An no one shows alarm.

So if it's food, or warmth, or sun you seek
Come along to here.
Where it's days, months, or just one week,
It's the 'Empire', just north of the pier.

■

Rainbow (Rondeau)
Geraldine Squires

Rainbow tinctures arching glow
Iridescent in their bow.
Azure in the heaven's blue,
spectrum in soap bubble's hue
mirror here on earth below
Rainbow.

Summer Explosion

Red of sunset's fiery glow,
autumn leaves of orange show,
greenest grass of Lincoln's hue
gentian of deepest blue
turning soon to indigo,
Rainbow.

Modest violets will show
purple heather swift will flow
over barren spaces new.
All will show their colours true
following in Nature's clue:
Rainbow.

∎

Laburnums
James Whalley

They met at dusk in the gardens.
A magic time - a scented breeze
and the silent, listening, laburnum trees
trailing yellow through the greying sky
and the clouded heavens.

Fleeting hope and falling shadow.
Fearing words would break the spell
they played their formal, mannered, careful game so well
each small advance a risk made of a chance
- too brief, too slight to grow.

Still life moves on, though framed in other ways
and passing years will soon dispel
the recollection of some half-forgotten thrill
until he sees, by chance one day, the trees;
the yellows - and the greys.

∎

Summer Explosion

Welcome To Summer
Jacqueline Claire Davies

Hallo summer, welcome
I've not seen you awhile,
Nut now you're here.
I know you'll make everybody smile.
With warm and sunny meadows,
Where cows and sheep will lay,
Hot and sunny beaches,
Where little children play.

Trees and flowers in full bloom,
Colours of every hue,
Everybody happy,
So many things to do,
Hallo summer. Welcome,
I hope that you can stay,
A little longer, this time.
Before autumn comes our way,

■

Summary
Josie Davis

Summer.... is a swelling of ankles,
an irritation of eyes,
a sneeze of dust.
It is a busyness of bees
and a worry of wasps.
Ants are everywhere
and on one day in the year
the air is a smother of wings.
Summer.... brings
Christmas catalogues,
hose-pipe restrictions
and a gaggle
of unfazed, double-glazedmen.
The earth cracks,

Summer Explosion

backs blister, and mother, father
brother, sister leave for Spain.
Australia retains The Ashes....
Summer.... is a PAIN!

(until - Winter comes around again!)

■

The Gymkhana
Winifred Heeley

Ready, steady
Willing and able
Are the horses
From the stable
Entering in
The gymkhana's fun
Willing to trot
Jump or run
Riders mount
All willy nilly
Hoping they
Will not look silly

Will they drop
Their egg from spoon?
The race is on
They will know soon
Then all eyes
Are on the sack race
Where riders hop
And horses pace
There's lots in store
Events galore
I enjoy gymkhanas
And want some more

■

13

Day Return
Stanley Bates

We had a good journey on the train,
And here we are at the seaside again.
Down past the shops and onto the pier,
It really is great now we are here.
The sun shines bright in a cloudless sky,
Bringing out colours to catch the eye.
Beneath the pier the tide is flowing,
Ripples and waves in the sunlight glowing.
The sound of children shouting with glee,
Splashing around at the edge of the sea.
The little boats go sailing past,
Bright white sails about the mast.
We see the swimmers bobbing about,
Some of them wave and give us a shout.
Along the pier we make our way,
We certainly are enjoying our day.
Men are fishing from the end of the pier,
They make a catch then enjoy a beer.
We stand there gazing at the waters hue,
And the seagulls flying in sky so blue.
On the horizon ships sail past,
They seem so still yet go so fast.
The hours fly by on this glorious day,
Now homeward bound we must make our way.
One last look as the sun goes down,
Spreading a glow all over the town.
It was only a day spent by the sea,
But it was golden for you and me.

■

Summer Explosion

The Gift Of Summer
Betty Bramma

Welcome summer, halcyon days and azure skies,
Scented flowers and gentle breeze,
Multi-coloured butterflies,
Sweet honeysuckle, bumble bees.

On leafy bough the blackbirds sing,
And honey bees their nectar seek,
And swallows swoop on velvet wing,
Whilst purple violets shyly peek.

Forgotten are bleak winter's days,
As nature in oblivion,
Soaks up the summer sun's warm rays,
And once bare trees their green cloaks don.

And in the evening's heady balm,
When crimson sun sinks in the west,
And all around is peace and calm,
Then nature takes her well earned rest.

■

The Season's Symphony
Gwen Mackay

Spring is like a Symphony
All light and fresh with showers
That sprinkles on the bulbs and wakes
The daffodils and flowers

Summer bursts through like an orchestra
Straus waltzes, guitars and strings
Which fills the air with sunshine
Scented nights when robins sing

It's Autumn and the music changes
As the leaves fall off the trees

Summer Explosion

The sounds of Beethoven and Litsz
Float eerily on the breeze

Winter is like the roll of drums
As the snow and pouring rain
The symbols clash and lightning flash
Upon the window pane

And so the seasons of the year
Each mood, each month doth change
Like life, it ebbs and flows
Till Spring comes round again

■

Sunburn
Linda Bull

I love to get a suntan and get my skin all brown
but then whilst I am burning I wished then I'd cool down
but when my skin starts peeling and it becomes quite sore
the colour of my skin then goes all red raw.
I've stayed out in the sun too long and now I sit and moan
the pain I get from my suntan all I do is groan.
If pain is all you suffer whilst you try to get a tan,
I think that I'd have rather stayed, as white as I can.

■

The View From The Hill
Joyce M Colton

The sunlit field of ripened grain,
Viewed from the height of green-clad hill,
Ripples, wavelike, in the breeze,
Obedient to its unknown will
And shadows, cast by passing clouds,
Across the whitened surface sail
Like ghostly galleons on a sea,
Darkening the visage pale.

Summer Explosion

Harbingers of death are they,
For soon, the reaper's sharpened blade
Will raze the harvest of this field
In summer fullness now arrayed,
The, stubble rooted in the earth
Will be consumed by cleansing fire
And heaven's winds will blow away
The ashes of the funers pyre.

Joyous summer, tinged with sadness,
Beautiful, yet bittersweet
As life and grain reach full fruition
In the bright sun's warming heat,
For when the darkening shadows creep
Across earth's whitened, waiting field,
Life's harvest of both wheat and tares
Must to the reaper's bright blade yield.

■

Blackbird
Wendy Dedicott

Tail erect in shiny black
Blackbird calls out a loud 'wack, wack'
His orange beak and sparkling eye
Warn the birds that danger's nigh
But later when it's all died down
He joins his wife who's dressed in brown
For worms they search and peck the lawn
Whether it's dusk or early dawn
They build their nest with care and skill
And hope one day with eggs to fill
They tend their young with love and care
And feeding duties both birds share
Then blackbird from on high will sing
Proclaiming that he is the king.

■

Summer Explosion

Booming Summer
Julie C Stoker

It's lovely when the Summer time's here
It fills everyone with so much cheer
The Winter miseries seem to fly away
And beautiful blue skies replace the grey
It's the season of holidays and that's just swell
When people are relaxed and feel really well
Flowers are in bloom everywhere in sight
And the beauty of every view around is certainly at its height
The seaside buzzes with tourists galore
While colourful boats bob along the shore
The Summer is indeed a wonderful time
Uplifting, joyful and utterly sublime
Cricket on the lawn and Wimbledon with strawberries and cream
You wish it would go on forever like some idyllic dream
So let the magic of Summer totally envelop you
And emerge from its soft embrace as fresh as the morning dew

■

Sun Day
Elizabeth Barkley

I sat in the garden today,
The sun was bright and gay,
The birds were chirping,
The spiders lurking,
Waiting for their prey,
The bees were busy buzzing
Dancing for their friends
To tell them where the treasure is
Before this fine day ends
The smell is on the air
of people cutting grass
The sound of aeroplanes on still air

reminds me of dusty London days,
there were no flowers there
but it had its own beauty
of shade and light, dust and heat,
noises of people laughing, crying,
Mothers shouting or crooning to their offspring,
the smell of pubs malty, smoky, raucous,
the lovely hearty accent of friendly cockneys
and the poor tramp the park and pavement home
all this because the sun shone today and took me home!

■

Nellie's Only Outing
(For Nellie Smith)
June M Blackwood

I have a tale to tell you, it really is quite sad
The moral of this story, makes me rather mad

I look after an old lady, she's almost eighty-six
She has a job to get about, but just manages with her stick

She lives alone in a little house, in the middle of our street
The neighbours come to visit her, they think she's rather sweet

She cannot leave her house you see because she has a job to walk
But she enjoys the visits people make, she loves to sit and talk

Her only outing is once a week, to a club she goes
But from next month this has to stop, it's the decision the council chose

So what has she now to look forward to, will she lose touch with her friends?
There's almost thirty in her club, on the mini bus they depend.

Summer Explosion

The special bus which picks them up is to be stopped by those who know
Now poor old Nellie and her friends have no meeting place to go!

No summer days out to look forward to, the future now looks bleak -
And how will those pensioners feel without one day out a week?

∎

Memories
K Toovey

Let me see the sea once more,
and view the mighty waves as they pound against the shore
If only I could taste the salty spray upon my lips,
And watch the waters rise, with foam along the tips,
'Tis many years ago, since I trod the golden sand,
Where I found those pearly shells, and held them in my hand,
I remember as I raced along to meet, the tide of swirling waters, which crept around my feet.
Oh, those halcyon summer days, when I was but a child,
Now, I'm getting older, and my thoughts are running wild,
Yet I still hope to see, those dreams again come true,
But, best of all, I dream of all those things I shared with you.

∎

Jewels In The Aegean Sea
Sally Coates

They are like sparkling jewels in the Aegean sea
islands scattered carelessly with calculated beauty
the sun reflecting it's own glory in the sea
and keeping the ancient stone altars warm
during the day and the resplendent moon at night

watching over her sleeping Gods and mortals
her beauty is mirrored in the sea, her light
reassuring the Greek Islanders with her serenity

They know that many crude tourists might
fleetingly trample on their Gods resting places
but that the Gods are safely out of sight
of people who do not know how to kneel
paying homage beneath pedestals made high
over the centuries by the Ancient Greeks who
prayed over and over but with a sigh
as if they knew what was prophesied for Greece

Now the Gods may be sleeping
but one day they will awake
and there will be much weeping
for all the Greek tragedies
that have been enacted by
their mortals while they slept
but they will not tell a lie
when they say that they're here for us now
towering high above watching over lovingly

∎

Tableau
Peter Williams

Evening draws in,
Pastel shades of Keats,
Seasonal mists and mellow drama
Produced by candlelight.

Wax figures in a landscape,
Painted oceans of tears
Falling on our knees.
Let us pray for rainbows
To end in pots of gold
(And silver spoons to stir our teas).

Summer Explosion

Leaves float in pools of fish
That swim in silence.
Broken statues
Posing questions
Of what to wear
And how to eat oysters
With pearls in your hair.

■

An Ode To Paul
(A fishy tale)
Lesley James

While sitting at his work one day
This man he made a wish
I'd really like in my backyard
Some Japanese Koi fish
In thought, he sat down at his desk
To write someone a letter.
But in his mind all that he knew
The bigger they were the better
He bought himself some weeny ones
But soon he wanted more,
And when he went to get them
Oh boy did Saunders score
He bought himself one 4ft long
And Sue said "No you're joking"
She shook her head and walked away
The fish and Paul were smoking
"Now come on Paul please calm things down
the kids and me do matter"
But all that Paul could think about
Was making his fish fatter
"Life is too short and all these fish
one day we'll all be dead"
Sue wished she hadn't said that now
As the fish sleep with them in bed.

■

Evocation
Jean D Mitchell

Why do holidays of long ago
Haunt us with such a rosy glow?

We now forget the boredom of the rain
Noses pressed against the window pane.
Nothing to say for a suggested letter,
Puzzles and card games scarcely better
Than going out and getting wet.
The long Dull wait until the teatime gong.

Nor do we recall that reckless run
Down to the beach to roast beneath the sun.
The agony that followed, day and night,
Sitting in shaded rooms, a ghostly white,
Daubed with calamine. Vest of lightest mesh
Could not be borne by that tormented flesh.

But what we do remember, clear and sharp,
Are first impressions, candles in the dark.
The smell of seaweed, gorse and thyme,
A struggling fish caught on the line.
Hot smells of pipes from fires just lit
After long months in winters grip.

Tumultuous footsteps on the stair,
Sand coated feet and salty hair,
Delicious feel of warm extruded peat
Between the toes, where footpaths meet.
And on the rocks the roaring sea
Rebellious, like the young and free.

■

To A Butterfly Found Dead On A Factory Floor
David O'Sullivan

When nature first kissed thee
You spent those hidden hours
under the leaves of the tree
safe from April showers.

When you were born again
your beautiful wings took flight
and the sun came from the rain
and there was a wondrous sight.

Amongst the flowers you played
fluttering with the bees
but then you went and strayed
and glided with the breeze.

You settled upon the stone
twitched, then spread your wings
for you were all alone
lost with foreign things.

Your beauty was designed
by loving hand and mind
its touch you hoped to find
but you flew tired and blind.

When dead upon the oily ground
your colours did not fade
'twas then my summer was found
knowing beauty's not man made.

∎

Summertime
Thomas Carroll

Cold night is the winters gun.
Now we have the summer sun.
Clear blue skies - beach fun.
Lazing - sleeping as the children run.

The sweet perfume of the 'Alpine Sink Garden'
Flowers red, yellow, orange and pink.
Lush green grass pleases the eyes.
Robins singing pierce the skies.

The music of the humming bee.
Enhances the fragrance of the sweet pea.
Like a chorus the flowering shrubs sway.
The gentle breeze is a melody.

Oh! those long summer nights.
Cruising in the car - what a delight.
Looking for talent - drinking beer.
Wolf-whistles - girls here.

It is only summer frolics
Meet a girlfriend and drink
Horlicks - 'coffee'?

∎

At The Red Deer
Krystyna Lejk

Heat of the day,
you can't have it here.
You go to the pub
for a pint of beer.

Summer Explosion

There it is hot,
smoky air, noise,
a kaleidoscope
of people, their voices.

A tangible atmosphere
entwined with your wishes
brings up the past,
our Valentine meetings.

Never mind the heat of the day.
You can have it here...
you go to the pub with him
for poetry and beer.

∎

Sings - Now The Summer
Malcolm Wilson Bucknall

Sparrows hop around the rain butt,
Splashing in the overspill,
Bright coloured flowers pepper gardens.
Kingfishers nest, by water mill.

Blackbirds voice their sweet refrains -
From hedgerows budding green,
Feathered echoes, flood the skies,
Cuckoos again are seen.

Crystal dew - sparkles the meadows -
Glistening in the light of dawn,
In confused patterns - starlings muster -
For ritual dances on the lawns.

∎

Summer Explosion

My Seasons
Sheilagh Benson

Snow covered branches bend in the breeze
crystal like cobwebs sway from the trees,
winters cold finger point to the earth
where soon the snowdrop will give birth.

Then follows the spring with flowers galore,
and daffodils bow welcome at your door,
the tulips, such a colourful sight
will warm the heart and give delight.

Then comes summer all gay and free,
to put new heart into you and me,
now see the roses, roof top high
which gladdens many an up turned eye.

When autumn comes in rustic colours
and bonfires burn and fires blaze
these are the days that I like best
the leaves of orange, red and brown,
to me are worth a golden crown.

∎

The Single State
Maureen Archbold

Those who accept the single
state in life
Jesus honours and applauds
for they are established
in their hearts
True companions of our Lord
they are single for
the king they love
Set free from anxious ties
and from a material
worshipped word.

They have a very special gift
Jesus is their goal
they walk the path of
Righteousness.
Giving all of one self
to our Lord.

∎

Even To The Dust
Robert Furze

...the True Church remains below
Wrapt in the old miasmal mist.
T.S.Eliot (The Hippopotamus)

I pass it every day, the church grown
from this earth, respectable
quiet eminence, arcane
mysterious receptacle

like a nightclub I once knew
a flashing neon converted church
with bouncers. But here it's day and no one's
about: going in; going out -

the cold detached needs nothing
to deter trouble. The label CULT's
enough; an apres-Waco
fear generated from the True Church

and the pulpits of the front
pages. But still the balloon inflates
nearer the point; expands, expands,
rubber scratched tight on breath; the pin.

Scraps of helium flames consume
the Cultists' and the True Church: windows
exploding from an inner violence.
After all, the two are fused: the blood that drives

is from the same source; interpreters
transubstantiate for their
own ends. And with publicity
make it palatable.

■

United Beach Mission
G Brownhill

It's 10:45 and I must run,
To the Beach Mission, it is such fun
I run and skip and jump and play,
And learn of Jesus every day.

The 'Aunts and Uncles' tell each one,
That Jesus is Gods only Son,
He came to this earth to live among men,
He died on the cross, then he rose again.

The 'Aunts and Uncles' tell us all,
That Jesus listens when we call,
That Jesus' love brings peace and joy
Even to me a little boy.

■

A Child's Delight
Jeanne Boffey

See the packing has begun
Now's the time to see the fun
We are off to see the sea
We're as happy as can be.

Books and pens are packed away
Spades and buckets rule the day
Now the car is at the door
Hurray! We're off to the sea shore.

Summer Explosion

Goodbye to the noisy town we say
'Cos to the country, we are on our way.
School is forgotten as soon we'll be
In a country cottage, enjoying our tea.

At last we arrive. The view is fine.
Forgotten is all we have left behind
As chickens wander about in the yard
And the 'Moos' of the cows can now be heard.

The ducks and the geese on the pond we feed
And we walk out with the dog on a lead.
We help with the milking early each day
And collect all the eggs that the chickens lay.
Our home is so distant - far away -
For this is a lovely holiday!

∎

August Holidays
Mary Marriott

The school holidays are here again!
Fun in the sun
For cheerful crowds with happy faces.
Queues in the rain
For pleasure Grounds and indoor places.
Children crying and demanding.
Parents shouting and reprimanding.
Everyone knows it's August again!
Lower prices and empty beaches.
Much more pleasure for leisure seekers.
The Autumn Term has just begun.
Now the 'Pensioners' can have their fun!

∎

Old English Summer
Dennis Malin

Oh comely wench what shall we do?
On this fine Summers day
Shall we to a haystack?
Where we can sport and play
Oh fair young maid when you have done
A bun upon your hair
Thither to the next town
To see the annual fair
Or shall we go a few leagues hence
Unto the bluebell wood
And stand upon the very spot
Where our ancestors once stood
Shall we gather pretty flowers
Garland or nosegay
Or list to the travelling players
Sing madrigal and roundelay
Beware footpads and highwaymen
As you travel to the village
For you are such a buxom wench
Just right for rape and pillage
Or shall we to the greenwood
To poach a little deer
Forsooth gadzooks oddbodikins
The Summertime is here
Prithee maid what shall we do?
As the sun doth shine just now
But you must take the yoke and pail
And milk the old brown cow
But we will court beneath the moon
For Summer night will be here soon.

■

Summer Explosion

A Garden
Irene G Corbett

A garden is a place
Where one can hide away
And forget about the troubles
That worry us, day by day.
The colours of the rainbow
Are spread before our eyes
And roses climbing upwards
As if to reach the skies.
Hollyhocks stand upright
Against the garden wall
And sparkle in the sunlight, beautiful and tall
A hundred different fragrance
Scent the summer breeze
While birds, bees and butterflys
Dart in amongst the trees.
The lawns stretch out like velvet
Upon which fairies dance
How glorious is the garden
Which sunshine does enhance.
In spring, a fresh new life, a garden will display
Daffodils, tulips gay, to brighten the cloudiest day.
Orange, gold crysanthemums
Berries, soft with dew
The leaves are turning brown
In autumns golden hue
Too soon, she'll wear her winter white
As another year is through
There's no place, quite like Gods garden
To see one self aright.

■

The Shore On Longboat Key, Florida
John Wedge

Conifer and cactus, palm and oleander
Clasped within the arms of the condominium,

Summer Explosion

Little lanes and stepping stones by the pool meander
Leading through the oat grass, leading to the shore.
Shattering of shells through a thousand generations
Handsomely created a beach of silver sand,
Daily tides contributing a changing decoration -
Open-book coquina, scallop, whelk and clam.
Mile upon unhindered mile lap the gentle waters,
Sanderling and dowitcher scutter with each wave,
Willet, gull and plover acting as supporters,
Turnstone joining in the frenetic to and fro.
Egret and white ibis contemplate the action,
Conscious of their beauty, while unending pelicans
Flap and glide in convoy approaching the attraction -
Fish, too small for market, tossed into the wind.
Overhead a frigate bird, elegantly soaring,
Waits to rob a seagull of her hard won prize.
Terns patrolling inshore, suddenly then boring
Down to seize the tiny prey, shake, and rise again.
Heavily a pelican emulates that capture,
Testing credibility, a creature of such size.
Sun and sea and scenery ingredients of rapture,
Lucky those who live on lovely Longboat Key.

∎

A Day To Love
W A Roberts

Sweet buttercup kisses,
and fields of yellow gold,
warm summer days spent,
with a girl that you can hold.

trees are slowly swaying,
to the silent song of a breeze;
a soft hand
held gently in yours...
that you so tenderly squeeze.

walking slowly through soft,
green grass,
that rolls as gently as waves upon a shore;
words whispered softly...
of loving you forever more.

...and while cotton clouds lazily sail by,
in china blue skies above.
you turn and tenderly kiss the sweet lips...
of the girl you will always love.

■

What Is A Summer's Day?
Jean Cunningham

Lying in a hammock,
Gazing at a clear blue sky,
(And occasional fluffy white cloud).
Listening to the tinkling sound
of a fountain nearby.
A long cool drink in ones hand,
Sweets - no chocolates they would melt.
A dog too tired for walkies,
Husband too sleepy for talkies,
Sheer bliss is a summers day!

■

Beauty
A Rogers

Go out, enjoy the sea and sand
Listen to the music of the sea
as it rushes towards the shore
The power behind the waves
The sand, so fine, yet stays behind
Feel the wind in your hair
- no matter the mess
Unless we feel the elements physically,

Summer Explosion

we cannot feel emotionally.

Learn to live with nature
You learn to live with self
The beauty of a flower can be achieved within our souls
It radiates outwards and the beauty from within
shows and draws like a magnet

How often a beautiful person to find on opening
their mouth this beautiful vessel is empty
Look into the eyes of the crippled body in the chair
What beauty takes one breath away
To learn to differentiate between
the two is a valuable lesson and
once learnt by many, would make the
natural beauty wish to achieve the inward
glory which is every mans right, not gift

■

Summer Flirt
T L Grandi

Sunlight edges the grass as the
Wind plays through the fields
bending and swaying, playing the part
but never totally yields.

Sun glistens on the hedgerows
Warming the life it holds
the leaves respond, buds unfurl
Protects from the heat all it enfolds.

fish bask in the river,
feeling the life giving rays
Swimming to and thro
never changing their ways.

Sunlight dipping her fingers
gently into the pool

rippling, shimmering, laughing,
generally playing the fool.

doesn't she realise the
spell that she casts
as she gently seduces us
down to the last.
hiding then peeping between the
leaves.
Plays like a temptress, and wholly intrigues
She knows her power as spring gives way
She knows her allure as she warms up the day.

■

In Abingdon Abbey Garden
Daphne Leete

Flower beds all spick and span.
Showing the dedicated work of man.
Copying God's creative way,
With a glorious display
Of flowers so cultivated,
That my spirits are elated.
Red, orange, pink and blue,
Green leaves and silver too.
Canopied by a blue sky,
And no grey clouds passing by.
A glowing sun, and slight breeze.
A background of magnificent trees.
While butterflies and birds fly by me,
And my eyes take in this glory,
The chatter of the birds cease.
In the Abbey garden there is peace.

■

Summer's Explosion
Jim Leonard

I remember the days
When Summer's explosion
Of colour and life
Thrilled me to the bone
And warmed my soul,
For nature's excellence
Was woven into the countryside,
And its flowers were strewn
For everyone to see,
And children played games
In the greenest grass
Whilst up in the heavens
The sky was as blue
As the most delicate bluebell
And the sun that shone there
Bade welcome to the world
And we thanked Mother Nature
For the treasures she bestowed.
And then towards evening
We sat around contented
As the sun slowly sank
In a pallet
Of brilliant reds
And we stood there mesmerised
As the sun said goodbye
And welcomed the first star
To protect us through the night.

■

I Walked In The Country
Ann Martin

I walked in the country today,
Seen all the trees on display,
lovely flowers of summertime,
And the peace was so sublime.

Summer Explosion

You could hear the birds singing,
Their songs on the air winging,
Summertime at last is here
To fill us all so full of cheer.
I remembered God's handiwork,
As I walked in the country today.

■

Summer's Song
Gwynneth Curtis

Growing pains are humming now.
Luscious fruits dip and bow -
consummation of Summer,
the orchestral success
access to life itself,
to life that is good
but life with a mean mood
of passions, regret and threat.
Scum and scab blotch and mar
Summer's delicious health.

Vigour flames from heat of sun
to fester this golden wealth
to perish and putrefy,
bleach and parch - suck dry
until a sultry signal warns -
a storm - charged to destruct
this harvest's holy credence,
coda to collapse of Summer -
prognosis for winter leanness
that is now Summer's greenness…

So Summer sings her song
before death - that is long,
death that is weak
and cannot speak.

■

Riding
D S Tallbot

Sometimes when I look outside
The feeling hits me like a tide
A sensation from deep inside
A yearning for a Summers ride
A need to be out under the sky
To speed below Nature's burning eye
A thirst to quench an inner fire
The open road a screaming tyre
This spirit cries from the heart
To accelerate to be a part
Of Summers thriving Human race
To ride the roads in winning place
For I crave for thrill and speed
And Summer days feed my greed
And I live for the adrenaline spell
And as to why only my bike could tell.

■

Outhouse Overture
Ron Wood

It's a beautiful summers evening
In the latter part of June
The stars are shining brightly
Only shadowed by the full moon
There is a very gentle breeze
Bringing life to the slumbering plants
Bouncing off the freshly cut lawn
And making the flowers dance
The air has a constant heat
Bare skin can certainly bear
No need for outer clothing
Wonders that are truly rare
No sign of busy animal life
On the ground or in the sky
They've had a fulfilling tiring day

And now in their beds they lie
We let these days just drift by
And take them for granted
The evenings are more precious
But seem finished before they started
If only they were longer
And I could sit here awhile
I know I'd lose my tension
And even afford a smile

■

A Lovely Day
Julia Yardley

A glorious day no cloud in the sky
As I sit in the garden wondering why
Some do not see the beauty around
The miracles of God that are seen to abound
The blue up above the green below
Butterflies fluttering to and fro
Flowers of every size and hue
Made by him for me and you
The scent of lavender near the door
The song of the birds as they begin to soar
Honeysuckle twining along the fence
A clump of fern green and dense
In the birdbath blackbirds splash about
It makes me feel I want to shout
Look around at all these wondrous things
See the glories that summer brings
Take time to reflect on what nature has given
Things that can bring you nearer to heaven
On a summers day.

■

Summer Explosion

Summer Days
R.H.H.

Down shone the rays and heat of a summers sun,
Raising a heat haze within the dunes of sand and grass,
That stretched as far as could be seen by human eye,
In bathing costumes we just lay there, you and I,
Browning and soaking up the sunshine,
Hearing the sound of the restless sea,
As it lapped along the shore,
Or listening to the wild gulls call.
At times we would rise and wander hand in hand,
Down the dunes and across the sea wet sand,
To wade or wallow in the sea, hiding our heads from sight,
Laughing in sheer delight,
As myriad's of glistening droplets of water each time,
Fell from us, sparkling and dancing like bubbles of wine,
Then back up the beach again, leaving our footprints to hide,
Beneath the waters of a lazy tide,
We picnicked midst the grass and dunes,
Then once more lay at rest, to find too soon
The golden sunlit rays had become,
A bright red ball, of a westering sun,
Colouring red the lapping waves and sky,
In haste we dressed there in the dunes, you and I,
Collected our things and ran for the bus,
In haste we left that hallowed sacred spot with sorrow,
But took comfort in the sunsets promise of another glorious day tomorrow.

■

Headmistress's Duty
Terri Ball

Apprehensive in the gloom of the staff-empty room,
Waiting for the parents of the Basher boy,
The Headmistress of the school,
Vegetarian and cool,
Sits waiting for the parents of the Basher boy.

Will they scream? Will they shout?
Will they murder with their eyes,
For how dare she criticise their darling one?
When she says he misbehaved
Will they knock her to the floor?
For they won't hear anymore against their firstborn son.

Every boy's mother knows he's unlike any other,
He's her conquering hero who can do no wrong;
Never lies, never hits, never steals, never spits,
Unless it was the other child that led him on.

Now he's standing by the wall,
An example to us all
Of the punishment incurred by those unsociable.
But we must not say he's bad,
Though he's violent like his Dad,
And enjoys bashing boys who will not do his will.

■

Louise
Helen Thomas

You were sent to me by God above,
A precious gift, for me to love.
My thanks I give him every day,
As I gently guide you on your way.
With your smiling eyes and golden hair,
You capture hearts everywhere.
As you now enter your teenage years,
It's harder for you to express your fears.
No matter what troubles may come your way,
I'll stand beside you every day.

Your joy in this life will be mixed with pain,
But without the heartaches, there'll be no gain.
Your path should be decent, honest and true,
That's my advice, but it's up to you.
Do a good deed, whenever you can,

Take pride in helping your fellow man.
This gift of you, I've had for a short while,
Whenever I see you, I have to smile.
Always remember, wherever you are,
That I am your mother, whether near or far.

■

Monstrosity Of Nature
Michelle E Smith

Medusa's in her den, lying in wait.
Her penetrating stare dwells upon her common source of prey.
They are enchanted with her silhouette;
That glares animation towards her dupe,
And are hypnotised with her smile,
That innocently mocks mankind.
But her fierce clasp
and unlocking talons,
firmly greet the messengers with consternation.
I know her prodigy,
She doesn't hoax me,
But her persuasive redolence,
Obscures the deep capability of this
monstrosity of nature.

■

How Can We Help The Policeman?
Charles Geddes

How can we help the policeman?
Our friend all dressed in blue.
Keep to the pavement truly,
That's much safer for you.

See the policeman in his car
Chasing after robbers
We can help the policeman
Tell him what we saw.

Summer Explosion

Keep our doors and windows tight
Do always what you know is right.
Go only with our friends to play
That will help the policeman.

■

The Human Race
Roy Cummings

The world is going mad and spinning
Very fast,
Everyone wanting first and no-one
Excepting last.
First past the post, achieves another goal,
Leaving some poor loser another long
Lost soul.
Getting to the top, is very hard
And tough,
And even when we get there it still
Is not enough.
We travel faster every day, and still we
Seem to lose our way,
And when we have to keep our date,
Always prompt, and still are late.
So if we all could just slow down,
And take life in our stride,
Life would not be such a race, but a calmer
Gentle ride.
Hold the world and slow it down, to stop
Everyone from rushing around
If we all could live less hectic ways,
Our future would hold better days.
So let's all get together and control
Our living pace,
And leave a better future, where all
Can live in grace.

■

Summer Explosion

The Seasons Of Love
Allison Magee

I laughed and lived and loved for you,
Yes, that was when our love was new,
Now our love has passed the test of time,
Yet I still want you to always be mine.

I remember when love was like a spring day,
Fresh and new all the way,
Now we've watched the seasons come and go,
Yet with you by my side I still feel a glow.

Autumn leaves and winter rain,
May batter at the window pane,
But love like ours will last forever,
And see us through to sunny weather.

■

On The River
A Humphrey

Two water rats were boating,
along the river Ouse.
They've found themselves a super craft;
a pair of old brown shoes.

A frog was on a lily pad,
to look at him he was so sad.
He was catching flies as fast as could be,
was so intent he didn't see me.

A kingfisher circled overhead,
waiting to dive to the river bed.
The fish were swimming to and fro,
wondering which one of them would have to go.

The wind was whistling through the trees
the grass was blowing in the breeze.

But on the river just the same.
The rat and frog were intent on their game.

■

Something I Said?
(The Chauvinist's Song)
Lawrence Stewart

How come you're always asking where I've
been, when I've got THAT look in my eyes?
Baby, if I told you, I think you
might be unpleasantly surprised!

How come you always want to know where
I am going, later on each night?
Baby, if I told you, you would know
and I don't think that would be right!

How come you're always asking why my
friends seem more important than you do?
Baby, I must tell you , my worst
enemy means more to me than you!

How come you're always saying that I
never bring you flowers anymore?
Baby, I remember. It was March
the fifteenth, nineteen-sixty-four!

How come you're walking out my door and
telling me you wish that I was dead?
Baby, I must ask of you.......
Was it maybe something that I said?

■

Artificial Roses
Kathleen Keywood

Roses of every shade,
Are but artificial made,
But a treasure seem to me,
Their beauty, is a joy to see.

Lemon, pink white and red,
Never do a petal shed,
Made with such a tender care
By someone, with a friendship rare.

Unexpected gift were they,
To a friend upon the way,
A treasure they will always be,
Because I may their beauty see.

■

Joys Of Summer
Marion Cox

Longer days, sunlit days,
The fragrant scent of flowers -
Lavender and honeysuckle,
Happy, carefree hours.
Time spent in the garden,
Strawberries for tea,
Butterflies flitting by,
Hum of bumble bee.
A day out at the seaside,
A visit to the zoo.
A picnic on the river...
These are the things we do
When we feel we need a break
From the cares of everyday,
When summer is upon us
And we ache to get away.
But we shall soon come back

To the dear familiar things
That mean home to us
And the blessings that home brings.
And now the dusk is deepening
To a soft, dark summer night
When bat flits, silent, overhead
And the glow-worm's light shines bright.
And so to sleep, perhaps to dream
As the dark hours slip away,
And we wake again to welcome
Another summer day.

∎

Oh Lucky Me
Josie Hickens

Gazing up into a clear blue sky
Here on a sunny beach I lie
Listening to the sound of the sea
And thinking 'Oh lucky me'.

Sea birds cries, close at hand
Hovering over the burning sand
Watching to see if I'm going to eat
Then share my picnic, what a treat.

This is what I came here for!
On three sides the mountains
In front just the sea
Again I think 'Oh lucky me'.

No chores today, just here to see
The mountains and the sand and sea
Completely relaxed, not a care
Again I think 'Oh lucky me'.

∎

Summer Explosion

Happy Romance
Vanessa Donald

Write me a poem
Drop me a line
Tell me I'm lovely
That I look divine

Give me a cuddle
Give me a squeeze
Give me a moment
I need to sneeze

Don't stop talking
Catch hold of my hand
Race me and chase me
Across the white sand

Under the starlight
Under the moon
Tell me you love me
That you'll be back soon

Smile in the sunshine
Laugh in the rain
Kiss my lips softly
And make love again.

■

Summer
Thomas Fitzgerald

Listen! What's that? The sound of the bees?
Or the bursting-forth of the buds on the trees?
Are those white crested blue waves that I see?
Or joyful June brides dancing with glee?
Are all things changing? - The people I see?
I think they are - between you and me -
There are smiles on their faces

Expressions less 'glummer'
The bees know the score -
The 'buzz word' is Summer!

■

Thoughts Of England
F G South

My thoughts just now are far away
To where the clear streams glide.
To where the squirrels go their way
To where the field mice hide.

They go to London's crowded streets
Survey the bustling throng,
And with a happy heart I greet
The folk for whom I long.

All these thoughts then are in my mind
While patiently I wait.
Until some transport I can find
To take me home in state.

And as I wait I think again
Of England's fields so green.
Of England's trees, of hill and dale,
A countryside that's clean.

I see a house upon a hill,
A village in the dale.
A place the soil our farmers till,
And drink their glass of ale.

As I ponder upon these things,
I, in the desert stand
But think not of the ancient Kings
Just England's pleasant land.

■

Summer Explosion

The Black Flower
Ellen W Worthington

I am a black flower
A sport among the true-to-form,
I spread my mourning petals
Among the shining throng.
I'm a gargoyle with the angels,
A skull in summer's tapestry,
Here, some say, I have no place.

Yet, for me there is no fading;
I shall be as now in winter's threat,
Unnoticed, black petals folding in repose,
A gentle sinking that does not wither.
My fine friends will fade and crack,
Their summer silks in funeral tatters,
While, darkly unchanging, to earth I sink.

■

A Brand New Day
C J Gregory

The sun is strong as she rises up
warming my heart and brightening my day
yellow in the garden from a buttercup
and a love in my bed that is sure to stay
oh! a brand new day
the joy from the birds is plain to see
the breeze in the air for harmony
the light in my life teases me
I guess I do not mind her company

Pale calm in the hills is all around
the green and the blue make a pretty hue
the cattle in the fields sitting on the ground
your touch is precious I am in love with you
oh! a brand new day
the milk on my doorstep is cool and fresh

the stream trickles down to my very feet
the feel of you a golden caress
a new day with you is such a special treat

∎

Memories Of A Lover
Joan Wilde

Red glowed the evening sky
on that hot day of July.
Red the poppies there in bloom,
and my heart sang to a lover's tune.
Soft the wind as you took my hand,
and we ran together across the land.
Bright the future looked that day
as we kissed in the meadow not too far away.
Pure the waters as we drank,
and you played on me a lover's prank.
Fresh the memory forever stays
of a lover I loved those hot summer days.
And now I remember as my feet touch the grass
and my hands touch the poppies as I pass.
I feel the warm air and watch the red sky
and remember my lover of days gone by.

∎

Fertility
Emily Beard

When days start to lengthen, and birds hop on sills,
We turn our attention, to winters ills,
The young embark on strenuous activity,
intent on retrieving their former agility,
and should their efforts prove successful,
subject themselves to measures more artful,
Attired to compliment what they've achieved,
they flaunt their assets on suitable ground,
where they feel themselves bound to find favour,

and maybe come into some affectionate behaviour,
Others contemplating some such advent,
bide their time till after lent,
when with dawn chorus alerting,
they follow their own style of conforming,
using equipment easily handled,
planting and fertilising at length tackled,
keeping to a strict routine,
within a certain borderline,
leaving sun and rain to serve their purpose,
nurturing what they mean to produce.

■

Dark Tunnel
Patricia Wynne

So many times I've felt
That I could not go on
Walking down the long, long road
My feet were set upon.

I've looked to left and right to see
If a turning can be found
Some respite from the weariness
The boring daily round.

The problems seem to stretch ahead
With no hope of relief
It seems there is no refuge
From my sorrow and my grief.

Then I look along this tunnel
And just within my sight
I'm sure I see before me
A tiny point of light.

Towards it now I stumble
For hope has sprung once more
Through the darkness

Summer Explosion

Which surrounds me
I see an open door.

My footsteps now are firmer
As I run towards the light
It was just a little turning
Which had hidden it from sight.

It was then that I remembered
God's word
Issued from His throne
If you walk the road with Jesus
You will never walk alone.

■

Whortleberry Pie
Abina Russell

I can taste it, tart, sharp, satisfying,
with fresh cream from the earthenware jug;
we had it in Summer holidays,
visiting grandmother's mountain farm.

We went by pony and trap, up steep
rough roads with gorse and purple heather,
there horned sheep and nimble goats grazed
and scattered wildly at our approach.
We stopped half way 'three miles' father said,
the pony drank from the mountain stream
and we climbed the fence to the meadow.

Uphill to grandmother's iron gates,
a brown and white sheepdog came barking,
and she running arms outstretched, welcoming;
she wore black, high buttoned bosoms,
high buttoned boots, grey hair in a bun.

"May we go and pick the 'whorts'" we asked
"they are best along the double ditch

Summer Explosion

take two milk gallons and don't be long;"
We groped for the dark purple berries
'mongst the leaves of the shrubs, short and strong,
we eat as we picked, our mouths stained purple,
"lipstick" said Tom, so we looked at each
other, giggling as we showed our tongue.

Grandmother had made the pie crust on
the wooden table, cleaned the berries,
then she put it in the bastable,
on a crane over the open fire;
"We'll have it for the tea" she smiled.

■

Double Summertime
Iris E Limb

Double Summertime
Double the sun
Double the pleasure
Double the fun.
Endless evenings
Games on the rec
Cracking tar bubbles
Jumping the beck.
Standing on your hands
Feet high up the wall.
Snobs and marbles
Or bat and ball.
Thick blackout curtains
To shut out the light
At bedtime. No fear
Of air raids at night.
Childhood memories
Innocence and laughter.
Double Summertime
Happy Ever After.

■

Nature's Trail
Roy Cummings

With knapsack packed upon my back
I'm off to hike the country track,
To pitch my tent beneath the stars
Lie down at night and gaze at Mars.

To arise in the early morning dew
Without a care as what to do,
Roll my tent and pack away
As I start to hike another day.

To get away and roam the hills
Enjoying nature's unspoilt thrills,
For the freedom of the open space
And wake each day in a different place.

Oh! To feel that mountain breeze
As I venture under the swaying trees,
To walk the hills and the dales
Across the meadows sweeping vales.

A leisurely trail all alone
Miles and miles away from home,
Far away from the human race
Strolling along at nature's pace.

The tiring day is almost spent
Time again to pitch my tent,
To dream away a perfect day
And start again, the hiker's way.

■

Harmony
Joyce Hamlett

Red poppies in a ripe cornfield
Sway in a summer breeze

Summer Explosion

Blue cornflowers their companions
Look down on wild daisies

Walking through a woodland glade
Tall trees, their leafy branches
Shelter green pastures from the sun searing rays
A wood pigeon calls to its mate
The startled rabbit runs to its burrow

Colourful barges on the river
Ripple the surface of the murky water
The moor-hen and her brood
Swim between the bull-rushes

Midday sun high in the sky
Bakes the mud under foot
As a solitary walker
Kicks up the dust
The drone of the bees, a distant shout of laughter
A prelude to life's harmony.

■

The Beachcomber
Sheila Owens

As I walk along the beach
With warm sand beneath my feet
I look across the sea and wonder
What lies beyond and yonder.

Warm sunrays reflect on the sea
Like mother of pearl sun beams
So delicate they could almost break
A vision that only nature can make.

In the distance dolphins play
Jumping for you on these glorious days
Calling out to one another one two three
Wouldn't it be nice to join in their spree.

Summer Explosion

Waves roll gently on the shore
Washing the sand and pebbles galore
Sea birds ride the waves with ease
Ducking and diving as the please.

When the tide turns and goes out
Children play, explore and shout
With excitement at what they see
When small fish in rock pools appear

■

Bank Holiday Monday
Lily Marsh

Reclining in deck chair
Enjoying my ease
Watching the magpies
High up in the trees
Savouring the fragrance
Of sweet scented flowers
Contentedly passing
The holiday hours.
A butterfly flutters
On gossamer wings
I marvel at Nature's
Most exquisite things.

All of a sudden
I hear a loud bang
A thud and a thump
A clash and a clang.
My neighbour is working
His face is all red
He's chosen today
To demolish his shed.
He lights a bonfire
Just for good measure
Spoiling for others
An afternoon's pleasure.

Summer
Sian Howe

Summer is hot with the chill of the wind,
of the soft subtle flowers that blow in the breeze.
The change of the night as it falls to an end,
The sunset that streaks past the trees and the Glen.

The morning is cold with a long stretch of light.
The morning is fresh, merry and bright, and the
Summer is hot with the chill of the night.

∎

Alfresco
Vera Charles

Push the patio door wide open
It's such a glorious day,
And the lawn that you trimmed this morning
Wafts fresh breaths of new mown hay.

We can eat out on the patio
Under the new parasol.
On chairs round the white plastic table
It feels quite continental.

The salad is deliciously crisp
And the mayonnaise superb.
It's amazing the difference it makes,
Just a touch of the right herb.

Well yes, now you've mentioned it, I can
Smell something like burning meths.
They've lit up their barbecue next door!
Burnt meat'll soon take our breaths.

What was that you said? I couldn't hear
Over that hover mower.
On no, a fly in the mayonnaise!
How those children yell next door.

Summer Explosion

They've set their mother off, and the dogs.
On the bread? A charcoal smut?
Oh dear, let's take our meal back indoors,
And pull the patio door tight shut!

∎

Tanfalier
P A Mela

Word has got around
There's bread to be had
At the isolated holiday cottage
Called Tanfalier,
Nine hundred feet above sea level.

Out there on a
Rickety bird table
There's bread…
Whilst low flying
Jet birds, who
Feed on oil
Disturb the place,
The feathered ones
Quickly and quietly
Chance their luck.

Behind the glass
Are photographers two
Taking holiday snaps
Of the birds
Eating the bread,
Who are disturbed more
By reflections than noise
And the dog who sleeps
In the sun
Which shines through
The windows of
The holiday cottage
Called Tanfalier.

Summer Explosion

Holiday Fortnight At Home
Stuart Michael Snowden

I do not think I like
Holiday Fortnight.
Everyone in gainful employment
Has gone away
To seek out enjoyment;
Gangs of children roam the streets,
Like animals
Searching for meat;
While the shouts of the stranded
Fill the air,
As if to make up for
Those elsewhere.

And I languish
In my Desert Island flat,
Expecting a postcard
To drop on my mat,
The postcard that read: "Wish you were here."

∎

Who's Got Sunburn?
P A Riley

Summer has arrived again,
Clear, flawless blue skies,
The whisper of a breeze, brushes my skin,
And the sun glares in my eyes.
My face flushes, in the heat of the day,
And my pale skinned limbs, redden and blush,
The air, warm, humid and dry,
Catches me in it's breathless hush.
A drowsy warmth, flows over me,
A sensation of drifting on air,
So tranquil, so dreamlike and calm,
Without a worry, a thought or a care.
Beads of perspiration, trickle down my cheek,

As the temperature continues to rise,
And a thin veil of freshness,
Passes over me, like angel sighs.
What peace, what joy, what bliss.
Smothered in warmth, from the sun,
In the heat of it's passionate kiss.
In the still, coolness of night, I tingled
Where the sun had laid it's claim.
I felt cold, and I shivered,
Yet, I still burned in it's flame.

■

Wishes Upon A Warm Day
Erica Donaldson

Let me soar with you, white bird
Let us fly
Far, far from here.
Can't you show me how
To transport myself to a different plane?
To think my unshielded bulk of human tissue
capable of elevation amongst the clouds
And, conjured by my own intention
To separate from my worries
Leave them imprisoned by gravity -
Speckled tombs below me, on earth.

■

Twilight
C Manning

The air is fresh, a sweet perfume -
of lilac floats by me,
new greenery and budding boughs,
I love this time of year.
Each bird so happy, not a care,
dark days have passed away
for a time, earth is rich again.

Summer Explosion

Twilight so warm today
that still I sit out in the dim,
as a noisy day is swept away
leaving room for peace at last
and now even singing birds cease.
Quickly dark and still descends,
there are no stars for cloud,
yet I could stay for another day
till the dawn wakes loud.

■

Only Just Sunbathing
Vicki Vrint

The garden -
A strip
of concrete - then brambles begin.

Milkshakes -
Not quite
But milk with some ice-cream stirred in.

Deckchairs -
So old
And broken - Don't sit down too fast!

But summer -
That's here,
With hot sun and daylight to last.

■

Goodbye Summer
Natalie Dale

Summer is when the flowers bloom,
Summer is when people enjoy themselves.

Summer is nearly gone now.. and the leaves
are starting to drop... Goodbye summer.

Love, Light And Warmth
S.G.O. Cook

Slender shining shafts of sunlight
Finding their way through the trees.
The sound of Nature's music
As the leaves are blown by the breeze.
The warmth around and beneath me,
The glory of the sun above.
Surely, in this wondrous summer
All nature must be in love.

The branches up above me,
Holding hands in ecstasy,
And the grass that's all around me
Uses softness just for me.
And then flying quite near me,
A lovely butterfly,
With the colours of the rainbow
That arches o'er the sky.

In a tree close by with leaves of gold and brown,
A blackbird sits upon a branch and then comes flying down.
Alights just there beside the tree,
Stays still and quietly watches me
Then turns around and leaves the ground
And flies back to the tree.

This quiet world I occupy
With the trees, the birds, the grass and sky
Seems to say, "We are just one,
All of us.
Happy to be in harmony
Beneath the summer sun."

■

Summer Explosion

The Dainty Blue Butterfly
Marilyn V Brown

I spotted a tiny pale, blue butterfly
As I was lying on the grass
Daydreaming one June afternoon,

It was such a pretty little thing.
It flew right over me
And landed in a fir tree;

I watched and watched,
Hoping it would come closer
To me, over the grass.

My waiting was rewarded, as
It landed on a daisy near the barn,
I squirmed closer and closer,

Keeping my shadow out of its way,
And I enjoyed a lovely view
Of such an attractive insect,

Hovering just off the ground,
Over the daisy patch.
All too soon,

The pretty, dainty butterfly flew off
Into the deep blue, cloudless skies
Of June.

■

Catamaran - Regatta Bound
Janis Priestley

Catamarans tossing on a sun-jewelled sea.
Twin hulls striving to set one another free.
Wind in the rigging making new sea songs,
And quiet down belong where quietness belongs.

Summer Explosion

A rattle as the sail is hoisted up our mast.
The jib flaps loosely as bigger yachts sail past.
The crew casts off and she lifts her gleaming bows
As, pennant fluttering, we set the course for Cowes.

The white hulled beauty slips deftly through the sea
Spray stings our faces making it difficult to see
The scents of ocean brine and of fresh sea air,
Mix with the odours of the galley's hot fare.

Relaxing far away from the thronging crowd,
We sit in the sun, singing shanties out loud.
Gracefully riding through the white crested waves.
Such perfect freedom makes us its willing slaves.

∎

A Midsummer Daydream
Ian Morrison

Sweet smells the fresh cut meadow
Overhead a skylark sings
Horses grazing happily
In the warmth that summertime brings
I cool my feet in a shallow brook
For a seat a grey stone boulder
A bumblebee humming to the rhythm of a grasshopper
The sun caressing my shoulder
Amidst this calm I close my eye's
Daydreaming of summers gone by
But every so often, interrupted
By a very persistent fly.

∎

Beach Party
Karen Tovey

Shining moonshine floods down on Carago beach.
Devoted couple slumber in dunes out of reach.

Summer Explosion

Rippling waves form whale gobfuls of saliva
and spits in onto the skinny-dippers and lonely diver.

Sandy toes rubbing together, grains
of sand and flesh enmesh with crabs brains.
A far-off disco beat pounds to the sea's heartbeat,
While singing couples wet and naked to the dunes retreat.

∎

The Year Abroad
David Caldicott

Lonely and frightened,
in a country unknown,
shy and retiring,
my courage has flown.

Far and distant,
seems the language I know,
all arms and hands,
is my communication show.

Helpful and friendly,
are the people I've met,
customs and ways,
I don't follow yet.

Weeks into months,
I soon find my way,
work and leisure,
now I've plenty to say.

Town into home,
the buildings are friends,
the community embraces,
the stranger who bends.

Time to depart,
a new role to play,

Summer Explosion

farewells are said,
as I go on my way.

I'm sad to leave,
the friends I have made,
photographs taken,
the memories won't fade.

■

Portrait Of Village Life
Diane Brookens

Remnants of yesterday's fair are seen
on freshly laundered village green
The sun is hot, the grass is parched
Geese stand still, stiff and starched

Sun beams on the pond briefly gleam
History seems to have become a dream
beyond a crumbling wall
where once the cockerel called
and the church lies in ruins

Beyond the cottage for 'To Let'
pubs nestle into subdued sunset
As villagers sup beer and ale
an old lady sits in her window, frail

Workmen brush off their dust and dirt
A young child falls and gets hurt
climbing a crumbling wall
where once the cockerel called
and the church lies in ruins

Painter and gardener argue the toss
about their master who things he's boss
White lambs dance to the song of Spring
Toddlers don't worry about a thing

Flower arranger sets out her stall
whilst intruding cuckoo takes over all
climbing a crumbling wall
where once the cockerel called
and the church lies in ruins

■

One Afternoon
Shirley Townsin

Deep in the English countryside
I took a walk one day
Come with me I'll show you
Things I saw along the way

A landscape spread before me
Mere words could not describe
Majesty and splendour
Right before my eyes

Gently rolling hillside
Meadows, trees, a brook
Horses quietly grazing
Lift their heads to look

Strolling through a leafy lane
A wood pigeon was there
I heard it gently calling
Across the summer air

And then a little muntjac deer
Cam peeping from the wood
I saw its face quite clearly
As cautiously it stood

Suddenly across the hedge
Came a cloud of gold
A dozen yellow-hammers
Lovely to behold

Time had given me a glimpse
Of something very rare
It was a glimpse of Paradise
Mine to keep and share

∎

The Day Tripper
Margaret Bennett

Twixt Whitley Bay and Gwbert
From Tenby to The Mumbles
Twixt Canvey Isle and St. Agnes Head
The train is heard a-rumble
The motor bike vibrates along
The charabanc the car
Ted is off to the seaside
And so is Ma and Pa
The anticipation of the cockles
Is at the back of the mind
The anticipation of the candy floss
The ice-cream and the donkey ride
Hurrah for the speed-boat
Hurrah for the pier
Hurrah for the sandcastles
Which will soon disappear
The tide keeps on turning
The waves flirt and twirl
Twixt Dundalk and Buckhaven
For each boy and girl
The sun is shining
The weather is fine
Hurrah for the seaside
Let us have a good time

∎

Maypole Dance 1959
Jennifer A Taylor

The school is neat and tidy.
It's the last week in May.
Blossoms gathered from everywhere,
to celebrate our special day.

Party dress for girls
Sunday best for boys.
Partners are chosen,
height matching height.
My partner's called Ashley,
he's handsome and bright.
Both feeling nervous.
Both feeling shy.
Tension mounts -
awaiting our turn
to skip on...

The maypole looks so pretty.
The May Queen has been crowned.
She sits upon her flowered throne,
watching the children dance around.

All hold our breath.
The signal's been given.
Smiles are exchanged,
as we each take our ribbon.
The sun appears as
we start the dance.
Both feeling smart.
Both feeling proud.
Tension fades -
roar of applause
as we skip off...

■

Summer Explosion

Summer Magic
June Madeline Archer

I get up early in the morn
Sometimes it's at the crack of dawn
There are so many things to be done
Life is just a bundle of fun
I'll greet the day with a smiling face
I'm ready to meet the human race
One's life takes on a different glow
Your movements become much more slow
You can stretch your body like a cat
I couldn't in winter - not like that!

The earlier I start there's more day for me
Then I'll sit down with cakes and tea
The dog sits and looks - he wants a walk
Just wait a few moments whilst I talk
I'll rush through the house to polish and dust
Suddenly everything seems a must
You can't hide the dirt on a summers day
Just thinking it's all gone away!

There's holiday brochures - we must have a look
We can't leave it too long before we book
We cannot agree on our destination
Walking hols for me holds no fascination
Can we settle for a tour
A trip to Barbados holds great allure
Well what's responsible for this transformation
It's Summertime in all it's Glorification!

■

Blessings
Nina Jackson

You planted me, dear Father God
In a little cottage filled with love
I have a cat and a lilac tree

And a mother and father so kind to me
You gave me the gift of hearing
You gave me the gift of seeing
The gift of smell of taste of touch
Dear Father God I thank you
For giving me, so much.

■

The Time Between
Norma Rhys-Davies

Where is summer? Shall we know it end to end?
Somewhere between January and sunset it lies
Waiting to be found
That we may honour our shining.

Each season fills its own time
Not carefully scienced by solstice or moon
But manmade - interlaced -
Occurring when needed.

Summer is for now-flowering
For feeling whole, for waking up, for letting go
Allowing bloomings to be seen.

It sneaks in unexpected with sounding heart
And cheeky flush and conjures
Coolness from the shade and winter
Transforming magic time.

It needs no gathering of accolades
Or show of recognisable wealth
Its only harvest is that of acceptance
Of who and what we are
And how we count.

Summer is simply being
Being shortly after - being not long before
Comfortable in uncertainty and

Summer Explosion

Bravely leaving nests to test the air
Which whispers in the gales
Or shouts in honeyed sounds - FIND ME.

■

Summer Is Coming
Peggy Jones

The blackbird finds the tallest tree,
And he sings in the evening rain:
His pure, sweet notes mean more to me
Than just another bird's refrain.

For Summer is a-coming in,
And Sol will warm the hard, cold earth.
The trees will dress in sparkling green:
The fire will die out on my hearth.

Then I'll walk bare-legged through the grass,
And I'll lie in its soft embrace.
So lazily the time will pass
With the hot sun on my face.

I'll saunter down a country lane,
And the bees will go bumbling by.
The wayside flora once again
Will delight both nose and eye.

But even when blue skies turn grey,
As they inevitably will,
I'll know, in spite of the damp day
That Summer is with me still.

The flowers I'll see from my room
Will take on a deeper hue, then
They'll glow like jewels in the gloom
As they drink in the English rain.

But I'll love every mood and phase,
Though I might shed a tear or two,
Remembering all the happy days
When I shared all this joy with you.

∎

I Remember
A K Jenkins

I remember those days, not so long ago
When one could wander, to and fro
Without fear, to stop and stare,
From Nature's wonder one could share.

Heaven's above, with evergreens so tall,
Earth beneath, Autumn leaves fall,
Tread along slow winding brooks,
Rooty banks, from their waters took.

Birds flying low, skimming the water's top,
Devouring flies resting, non-stop,
Scented fragrance, flowers sweet
Carpeting earth, so near my feet.

The bending path across a meadow runs,
I follow nature's having fun!
Silent beauty reach my soul!
Here! No man as yet played foul.

The sun falls low over the Western sky,
Reddish beams from its source, out fly,
Nature is tinged with red
Daylight! preparing for its bed.

Pause, gaze, tranquillity of scene once more,
Turn my steps towards distant shore,
Time with nature, spent today,
Life enriched, Oh! happy day.

Summer Explosion

The Jewel
John Seels

Today I saw the rain.
It fell like jewels and made me richer.
It felt wet
Yet soft and warm.
And when I came to taste it;
It tasted pure.

And the moon came down
like some sacred clown
And, whispering she told me to dream.
"Coz if you don't you'll miss the boat."
That's what she said to me.

From behind the clouds
the sun came out.
With her smile she painted a bow.
And with these words she made me cry;
"Love's all you need to know."

■

You Fresh Optimistic Thing
P J Mannion

Frost lays lightly on the ground
yet flowers blossom all around.

A chill is in the air as the wind blows through my hair.
Summer is in the air.
The frogs are leaving the pond and the rabbits jump with
joy.
Summer is in the air.

Still is the morning dew,
Birds sing their song in tune.
Summer is in the air.
Welcome summer... You fresh optimistic thing.

My Cappuccino Love
Daphne Chappelle

Bougainvillaea in Amalfi
Sunlight on the sea
Romeo, in a white apron
Making eyes at me.

High above the red-tiled roof-tops
We climb the grassy hill.
Mother, father, sister, me, to lunch
In the posh hotel.

Frangipani and lilies
Perfume the summer air
As he sets Ambrosia before me
Bliss beyond compare.

I twirl spaghetti round my fork
I've really got the knack,
"Heaven senta you here", say Romeo's eyes,
"Donta never go back".

He brings ice-cream in a silver dish,
Lingers by my side,
"Cappuccino?" he asks, but his eyes express
Molto, Molto beside.

Ah, memories of Amalfi,
Sunlight on the sea;
Romeo, in a white apron
Making eyes at me.

■

Summer Is To Me
David Wicking

A cock pheasant calling at the break of day,
the sweet scented air of new mown hay.

Summer Explosion

A lane with hedges and tall trees above,
sunlight through the branches, a cooing dove.
A park with lovers wandering hand in hand,
and peacocks proudly spreading tails so grand.
A village green - a weekend cricket match
where someone yells "He's out - a perfect catch!"
A river bank where slender willows grow,
and eager youngsters learn to punt and row.
A ripple on the water as hungry fish rise,
a lily patch with hovering dragon flies.
A woodland, where startled rabbits scamper
back to warrens safe from the hunter's gun,
and squirrels frolic in the midday sun.
A meadow hushed and still where cattle graze,
a trickling watermill left from bygone days.
A harvest field with rows of yellow corn,
deep bracken in the copse - a deer and fawn.
A pond, where little boys in welly boots
bring jam jars in search of frogs and newts.
A quaint old tea room by a running stream,
a pot for two - scones - strawberries and cream.

■

Summer By The Sea
Eunice Watcham

Holiday makers eagerly pack
To reach their destination
Some choose to drive or take a bus
Some travel from the station

Their tanning bodies line the beach
Others paddle in the sea
Whilst some prefer a shaded spot
Underneath a sheltering tree

Some stroll along the prom and browse
Amongst the seaside shops,

Buckets, postcards, hats and spades,
Not forgetting cool ice pops

Donkey rides and slot machines
Hats with "Kiss Me Quick"
Cockles, muscles, jellied eels
Or candy on a stick

Upon the pier, the big wheel turns
The ghost train screams aloud
Bumper cars crash to a halt
Whilst side shows draw a crowd

Then gradually they dwindle
As another sun goes down
The nightclubs and theatres are waiting
To say "Welcome to our town."

∎

Welcome Visitors
Jeannette Ashley-Green

Winter was cold, the nights were getting long,
I had only the robin for company and his winters song.
There in my garden, he sang with all his heart,
Perched there proudly with his red breast so smart.

Winter's a lonely time, visitors rarely call,
So to me all were welcome, even creatures great and small.
But soon came the springtime with natures new life,
Into my garden, came a blue-tit, with him his new wife.

They ate from the bird-table the food I placed there,
Such a beautiful sight, just to see this happy pair.
But what's happening? What's this I now see?
This couple have decided to share their life with me.

For up on the garage, a stately birdhouse hung,
And this loving couple knew their task had just begun.

Summer Explosion

Every minute of the day, they worked without rest,
Bringing the ingredients needed to build their fine nest.

Then, nature told them, that time had now come
For this pretty new wife to get ready to be mum.
Her true love fed and tended her with gentle loving care,
Helping to support the family they both now share.

The constant feeding, flitting to and fro,
Bringing worms and tit bits to help your babies grow.
Then comes the day when you teach them how to fly,
When the last one takes to its wing, it's time to say
"Goodbye."

Nature calls you to migrate today,
To a land overseas, somewhere far away.
I hope next year, you'll return to raise a family new,
Your life you shared with me, for this I say, "Thankyou."

■

Summerland
Rosemary J O'Neil

The world at last a better place,
We find joy in the gift of living.
People seem so different now,
Sincere and friendly and giving.

Each new day we are greeted,
By the warmth of the summer sun.
The gentle breeze that surrounds us,
Seems to provide energy for everyone.

A choir of birds sing loudly,
Rejoicing in the birth of a new day.
We join in their celebrations,
All that's living, feeling the same way.

Summer Explosion

A colourful array of flowers,
A symbol of the time of year.
The scent they give so pleasing,
To nature we feel so near.

Children happy and smiling,
Building castles in the sand.
We all share this love of summer,
For we're all in summerland.

■

Sunshine In The Rain
Andrew Hudson

When I get so afraid
and feel so alone
all I have to do
is just turn my heart toward home

When I need to be held
And feel your precious love
All I have to do
Is look to you, Father above

Because like sunshine in the rain
You're there to ease the pain
I really need to know
How much you love me so

When I seem so far away
And nothing is going right
I know that you'll find
A way to put me right

So when you feel afraid
Because no-one seems to care
All you have to do
Is believe that you'll find him there

Summer Explosion

Because like sunshine in the rain
He's there to ease the pain
He wants to let you know
How much he loves you so.

■

Summer Bliss
Mary Mycock

Swallows diving low, twittering loud
Clear blue sky, soft white cloud
Strong hot sun, beneath folk lie
Colourful dragonflies darting by

Bees humming on flowers neat
Dry dust, hot pavements up the street
Girls in pretty dresses long or short
Lads whistle, all good sport

Sticky tar, roads melted by the heat
New mown lawns green grass so sweet
Balloons floating above in fine weather
In the hot lazy days of summer

■

Unborn Child
Marion A Murray

Here am I
A child unborn,
I only live to die.
Still I wonder why...?
What have I done that merits death?
I have not drawn a breath
Of air, and yet
What do they around me care?
I lie in a bath of gore
That once was me.

Summer Explosion

My legs are slashed,
My blood runs free.
Perhaps this world is not for me!
This cold steel dish does not comfort me.
It welcomes death,
My death I see.
I would pray to God
Like She did pray
But I cannot.
My breath
Departs.
In pain
I cry
Then
I...

∎

Midsummer Lane
Jane England

In Turfpits Lane it's summer time, but will there ever be
A lane edged in hawthorn,
White lace parsley, comfrey,
For others still to see?
A road now runs where the lane winds narrow.
Here rabbits romp,
Squirrels still play,
Oblivious of lorries' thunder, while a sparrow
Chirps above its nestlings, impervious to the din.
On a bank a fox suns itself, but cannot know
That when this summer's done
The lane's gone, too -- into the bin --
Under the crush of the Northern Relief Road,
The loveliness lying,
Buried and mute,
Beneath its tarmac load.

∎

Summer Explosion

The Stream
Martin Brazewell

Gargle, gargle. Look!
See this leaf I've took

Babble, babble. See!
I'm shimmering under this tree

Splash, splash. Hear!
Me hissing along bright and clear

Plop, plop. Listen!
I chatter and I glisten

Splosh, splosh. Feel!
I'm wet, writhing and real

Drip, drip. Smell!
The dampness of a stream in a dell.

■

Life
Charlotte Anne Norman

Where is the future for these young of our
No job, no hope, they stand for hours
At corner ends and in the mall's
Oblivious of rain and snow that falls
They tread the streets evoking pity,
Then hurry back to cardboard city
Some choose to live this way we know
But some have nowhere else to go.
They lives they live are such a chore,
Whatever they do, has been done before
As they go through this vale of tears,
What ever's happened to their wasted years.

■

Memories
Patience Guerdon

The sun shimmers on the stream,
The ripples on the water gleam,
To skim which pebble will I choose,
Lying there in their varied hues.

The squelchy sand between my toes,
The salty smell tickles my nose,
The waves lapping on the shore,
Leaves memories forevermore.

The sun that filters through the trees,
The warmth of the gentle breeze,
The birds that sing and flit about,
The children's' laughter as they play and shout.

The long climb up the rugged hills,
Worth it for a view that thrills,
The care and worries left behind,
The peace and stillness let you unwind.

In the field I stand,
Surveying the surrounding land,
Crops growing, animals graze,
Peaceful in the summer haze.

Memories of past summer days,
Places, people, sunny rays,
In the treasure chest of my mind,
Look in yours, see what you find.

■

Summer Explosion

The Environment
Margaret Meek

What's happening to the birds and bees
What's happening to the flowers and trees
The disappearing of the hedges
And no wild flowers on the verges.
I've seen golden corn splashed with red
But now the poppies are poisoned dead
The animals too, are on the brink
Of soon becoming rare or extinct
So please remember, be aware
These living things are in our care.

■

Butterflies
Martin George

We lay in lush green
Hands dawdling in a lazy stream under a high sky
A sky that promised to be blue for ever and for ever
and for ever.

And stepping stones and clear water.
We were as children: so happy; so content and we
thought we must be in love
We watched two beautiful blue butterflies.
Exotic, fragile, of no possible consequence, darting in
tandem
Inches only above soft water.

No warning! A cloud, a darkening sky. The sharpening
breeze, cuts, ripples the water.
And for the briefest moment: the tiniest pause in eternity,
my butterflies come together.
I swear they kiss.

They part in the strengthening breeze.
Light blue wings fighting frantically to push them

Higher and hopelessly.
Then they are gone.

I wonder if my blue butterflies will ever meet again.

■

Moon
Gemma Parkes

She climbs the silver staircase
Of many winking stars,
To take her place
As Queen of the night-time sky.
Her shining face
Looks down from high
To watch her world a-sleeping
Gentle slumber breathes its silent lullaby,
Humming sweetly.

Moon is a distant lantern
Lighting the way of passing ships.
The lapping sea glistens
In moon's steady glow:
Nothing escapes her peaceful eye.
And when dawn is nigh, she sleeps;
Her face is barely see at day.
She bids farewell to all, till dusk,
When her time begins again.

■

Our Family Motto!
A S Sanderson

"Mummy, can I have a drink?"
"Biscuit, bread, cake under sink?"

"Mummy, will you play with me?
Is it time for lunch or tea?"

Summer Explosion

"Daddy, listen while I talk!
Can we go out for a walk?"

"Mummy, can we go to the zoo?
To buy some sweets, or to the loo?"

"Mummy, can we go to Granddad's to play?
Don't go to sleep! I have something to say!"

"Daddy, I have to get up in the night?
To let you know when it gets light!"

"Mummy, you're not listening again,
I can stand on my head and count to ten!"

The motto then has got to be
If it breathes, it serves the tea!

∎

Where, Oh Where Is The Summer?
Susan F Handoll

The summer house is cleared
Sunhats, panama and straw are ready
The parasol is mended
But where, oh where is the sun?

Bundles of brown fluffy feathers
Feed on scattered seeds
Already a first brood of sparrows
But where, oh where the warm breeze?

Some swallows flew over weeks ago
A cuckoo was seen from the train
The swifts have returned at last
But where, oh where the blue sky?

Pretty skirts and short-sleeved shirts
Hang ready, while we are back

Summer Explosion

In two jerseys a-piece and scarves
But where, oh where is the warmth?

Oh the flowers are out, the bees are busy
A few butterflies are on the wing
A caterpillar has eaten the red-currant leaves!
But where, oh where is the heat?

We should, by now, be able to say:
With long sunny days unfolding
From brilliant dawning to sunset's blast:
"Here, here at last, is the SUMMER."

∎

Burning Strawberry June
Edouard Tanguy

Wild yellow gorse sparks
pulses the blue air.
Across the immense musical green interlocking tapestry
the bee flights
through the structures
of mauve pollen.

As the butterfly,
on the stunned afternoon heat about us,
deep in the sun flower fires.
In the air-gloved silence of the crystal meadows;
spider webbed buds burst.
under
the sun's
disc

A trembling liquid gold.

∎

Summer Explosion

The Summer Morning
Sylvia I Moore

We slip from the stifled summer night
Into a clean, bright day
And open the door to welcome in
The summer morning.

The Morning Glory on Pergola'd patio
Trumpets a proclamation of colour to the sun,
And entwines with Clematis and Rose,
Celebrating the summer morning.

Bees fuss into honeysuckle, busily awake.
A Blackbird hops over the lawn
To find stretching worms in the dew soaked grass,
While a clumsy Woodpidgeon clowns on a rooftop.

And we sit here and watch
Unfolding Natures wonders
Sight, sound and smell
All in one beautiful Summer's morning.

∎

Loneliness
Maureen Archbold

Loneliness is the devils
biggest ally
He uses it to make people
sad, alone, looking out of
flat windows, where even getting into
a lift causes dread or going
up stairs, looks like a prison.
These great concrete buildings
so deprived of love.
These people once lived in
little old houses
with back gardens they loved.

Some lonely people, live all alone
just in a bedsit room.
Some have families but they
are forgotten because they are
just getting older.
They hardly see Grandchildren
they dearly love,
but there's no time
for caring for someone
who can't keep up the pace anymore.
There's no children's stories
or tucking them in bed anymore.
Loneliness though can be gone
by trusting in Jesus Christ
He never leaves lonely people
he comforts them and cares.
For who can be lonely
with Jesus your fried
for evermore.
A few are lonely who can't get about
Have a little dog or canary or a cat.

∎

Summer Fever
Ellie Langley

One day each year since I was twelve,
As the temperature starts to climb,
I'm struck by one of summer's
Unmistakable warning signs.

A niggly tickle inside my throat,
An itch in either eye,
A sudden sneeze, persistent cough,
It always takes me by surprise.

After winter's many coughs and colds
Brought on by damp and breezes,
There is no rest for many of us
Who suffer the summer's fevers.

Summer Explosion

I see a lawn that's just been mowed,
I shriek and run for cover,
But it's too late, the damage is done,
The fever's taken over.

My puffy eyes and streaming nose
Bear testimony to all others,
That I'm one of summer's pitiful souls,
Known better as hay fever sufferers.

■

The Jumble Sale
Karen E Poad

Roll up, roll up, for the jumble,
Lots of fun and rough and tumble.
All the bargains, you can see
T-shirts and skirts for fifty 'p'.
Come on in and look around
A bag full of junk, all for a pound.

Now, now, ladies, please don't fight
Tugging at dresses, with all their might.
Trying on skirts, shoes and jackets,
Searching for vases and tennis rackets.
Jumpers flying through the air
Crowds of people everywhere.
Clothes hanging on a rail,
The odd picture, hooked on a nail.
A toaster and a cricket ball
A small rug, ideal for the hall.
A handful of ties
And some books about spies.

It's all over by half past three
And the helpers drink their cups of tea.
The cash is counted for every stall
An excellent day, all in all.
Then the tables are put away

Summer Explosion

Until we decide on another day
To follow the bargain trail,
To our wonderful Jumble Sale.

■

The Dream
Debbie Hipkiss

So long till we can be together
All this time it seems like never
I want to be there with you now
But deep inside I know there is no way how

I close my eyes and all that I see
Is your laugh, your smile, and your love for me
My love for you grows stronger day by day
And my promise to you is I'll never take it away

I know that all I'm doing is dreaming
And right now I really feel like screaming
But if I scream I will beat that dream
The one about being with you always.

■

In Eternity's Sunrise
(To A Prophet)
Stuart Cross

Though she weeps beneath the morning star
- Her dewy web to weave -
And schools her rule of thumb afar
For every little entity

The mirth of summer wails
- The brightness passing fades -
And in its loom He lopes the hills
That bind us all in shade

Summer Explosion

(A silhouette He sings as softly as the breeze)
"Oh but the darkness of dread shall pass into wonder"
And Wonders Never Cease!

Though the strands of colour cheered me
As they pierced the clouds at evening
I still felt a hammering
On my heart lost and grieving

And the strands of colour faded
As they fell from sight cascading
Then I felt a belt of longing
" 'Twas all of us belonging"

Sang then the breeze to me:
"Oh but the darkness of dread hall pass into wonder
And wonders never cease!"

∎

Childhood Memories
June Turner

What happened to those long summer days
That wonderful carefree childhood phase,
It seems distant now, so long ago
And yet in my mind it isn't so.

I remember with joy the little things,
Paddling pool, sandpit, even the swings,
A jam jar with string could be home for
Butterflies, or fish and so much more.

Ice-cream cornets, lollies on a stick,
"Mind it's melting - come on eat it quick!"
Parma Violets a favourite too
Bazooka Joe Bubblies, stick like glue.

Punnets of strawberries, sticky cream,
Plastic sandals, to wade in the stream.

Days which were filled with laughter and fun
Those long summer days, with brilliant sun.

∎

After The Fire
Anna Parkhurst

The soft steps of night
Close in like the owls' soft feathers.
Deliberately, one needs the light.
This is how minutes measure
The scream of the human being
Who has no mental sight.
It's like the going out of the light:
The wall of ignorance, and dying.
Don't just see the face
Hiding pain and fear
Like curtain of lace
At him who jeer.

Now knowing that life is more than a game,
A shadowy line,
The dull gilt round the picture frame,
The reflection sad, features without feelings
Of the mind that is tame.
So, little lambs, don't die:
Play in the owls' moonlight.
Don't let humans sigh
Because their race and yours
Are saying a sad goodbye.
Goodbye fire, welcome safety.

∎

Summer Explosion

Raspberry Ripple
Maggie Harris

smiles hang like honey melting over fences
rinsing polar creases out of elbow joints
and stacking British reticence
like hyacinth bulbs

and the ripples run

on into the next street
where recognition stirs
and takes the place
of counting empty bottles

raspberry ripples into vanilla,
into chocolate
into black cherries
into neapolitan
into cosmo
into cosmos
into cosmopolitan

smile melt like honey
dripping from a hot fence
where summer ripples lift the lid
off British reticence

∎

Summer In Andorra
J R Pietrusiak

Splish, splash!
Wheeeeeeh!!
It's a downpour!
Oooh! A river through my tent!
Quick - perch on my rucksack!

Summer Explosion

Five minutes since
We were in paradise
Hot, sleepy summer
Fragrant, pine filled nostrils
Mountain glades, dappled shade
Mountain pastures
and barbecue picnic of fresh omelettes
sizzling in butter

and peaches, juice sweetly running
down chins and forearms
Mmmmmmmm....

Crach...Clickkkk...Brummmmmm!!
Livid flashes dance around the mountain peak -
and again - kraaaaaashhhhh...!!
The very earth trembles......

Phew! It's topped. Peace
The earth crackles and splutters as
rain soaks in -
Grasshoppers - grey leathery,
green velvet-bodied, hop gingerly -
The sun peeks round a cloud....
We are warm again.

■

Prairie Sunrise
Sandra Janssen

Pink colourstreak
Blurs
Amongst thistledown clouds.
Night drifts into dawn
Gently lapped by the sun.

The newly warmed prairie wind
Passes through the coarse grasses
On its endless search

Summer Explosion

For something unknown.
The sound of whispering grasses
Is broken only by the rhythmic rasping
Of grasshoppers.

Sun overhead
Intense heat
Shimmering stillness
Nothing
Until night.

■

Summer Sun
Daniel Healy

Sitting under the
cool summer forests
just watching dappled sun
as it trickles, gently
through my fingers,
you always knew
the way, intoxication
in sunshine wine,
it's my dream, every day,
at midnight another
summer

Now remembered
the cool grass
the warm blood
and innocence.

■

A Scene Between Two Trees
Brian William Ewan

Sunlight shining through the trees
The wisp of a slowly moving breeze
Birds, busily at song
Among a group of far away leaves.

Sparrow and Magpie twist and fly
Others simply pass them by
As they replay their age old game
For supremacy of the sky.

A heat haze on a dusty path
A Woodpeckers natter nat
Shimmering glimpses of young and old
Carrying their heavy picnic pack.

Flowers of yellow, blue and white
Butterflies, bees and wasps in flight
A blanket formed upon the ground
Its long blades green and bright.

A child laughing, a dog at play
On this drowsy summers day
Later on a cold ice-cream
To finally complete this scene.

Evening comes as evening will
All that moved will now be still
Bringing on the cooler breeze
Leaving only nodding trees.

■

Nasturtiums
Rosa Johnson

They are the prostitutes of my summer garden.
Bawdy and brash,
Gaudy and glorious.
Voluptuous in their moss-lined hammocks,
Trailing sultry shades of orange and ochre,
Alluring, making passes.
Flaunting themselves on the rockery,
Laughing and winking from their unmade beds
In startling shades of vermilion and gold.
Constantly returning to mock me on the gravel paths.
Passionate and promiscuous,
Taunting me, tempting me,
And I submit.

■

Summer Explosion
Helen Bryant

At first, faint warnings -
the sky paled, there were gentle flashes.
My aunt called them "summer lightning."
There was a distant roll of drums
as if a tribe was gathering for ceremony.

Suddenly great forks of light
tore the sky, stabbed our hearts.

I was staying in the country
at my aunt's house
with its big range in the cosy kitchen
where we were having teas, but my aunt stopped,
jumped up, spread a blanket
over the steel fender.
Close by, a thud - our elm tree?

Summer Explosion

Next day was calm and sunny.
People hopped, met, chattered:
a fireball had sped through the High Street!

We discovered a fallen branch
and a black scar on the trunk of our elm tree.
A great sky god had been angered -
the god Thor?

■

Crowned In Glory
Bernadette Higgins

At ten years old I waited for Neptune.
I the majestic beach queen
Soft sand my throne
Billowing breeze my crown
Sunblest goosebumps my gown.

The sun split through the sky
Shimmering fingers of quivering stratas
Warming to calm her fretting disquiet.
Slipping silently, sliding to kiss,
Red lips caress her ebbs to sigh.

I watched; waited, lulled by the lapping.
The lolling clouds rolled to whisper
silence. The slow sun sunk
As the waves swung their hypnotism
Crimson sojourner sinking to rest.

Down dissolving together, dipping down.
Awesome in their power, my smallness crouched,
Basking in my frailty.
Satiated I watched, snuggled in the sand.
My earth, my sky, my sea, my land.

■

Summer Explosion

The Urban Princess And The Peony
Karen Crawcour

The peony lay in superb disarray,
the sun beating down on its head.
The princess, nearby,
dumbly worshipped the sky,
her nose and her cheeks turning red.
The blossom, unbound, lay flat on the ground,
its beauty too great to support.
The girl lay replete in the fine morning heat,
her mind quite untainted by thought.
These voluptuous flowers lay basking for hours,
with all inhibitions released,
but later on, in their beds,
their frivolous heads
were both somewhat
browner and creased

■

Valley Of Song
Phil Powley

I watch them climbing up the slippery
slope of the deep coomb, seeking some
level spot to lie upon; he stooping
beneath his pack, she following on.

The chalkgrass slopes tumble like
rapids to the valley floor down which
a cart-track jolts: and at the highest
point of noon the shadows fall straight
down to shelter under basking oaks; and
hawthorn bushes on the rutted flanks
cage choirs of fluting nightingales.

From every bush the rising harmony
of song soars from a quivering orchestra
of throats: blackcap and whitethroat,

Summer Explosion

nightingale and wren, each one competing
to be heard. At every level safely
grazing sheep shear the white-dusted
grass, and crop with unenvironmental
lips and rockrose and rattle, orchid
and buttercup.

The lovers, for that is what they seem,
have reached a grassy ledge from which,
hands linked, they watch high summer
bursting into flame.

■

The Golden Burst
Gwen Mason

Oh dear, Oh dear, I am so very late -
In preparing work for the Summer Fete.

I meant to make this and jams of that,
But spent all my time in my gardening hat.

I hope Mrs Brown you'll forgive me dear -
You say it's too late to enter this year?

Now just look at my garden, it is a dream,
Yes I'll give you a cutting of Rose and Cream.

What's that you say, I should enter a flower?
Oh, which to choose, quite beyond my power.

Oh drat, there's that digging old cat again
Now look, it's coming on to a heavy rain.

The rain it spoils the blooms you see -
One day better organised I hope to be -

the golden burst you've got your eye on?
I can't enter that... it's a dandelion!

Willow Patterns
Colin Grindrod

Beautiful willow, weeping constantly,
what are you weeping for?

The river banks that you bind together
rely wholly on your strength of purpose.
Your youthful limbs are so supple and long.
Catkins, pendular, light as a feather,
dangle, spiralling along soft branches
which unfurl into a sprung umbrella
of bluish tinted, lamellar leafage
that mirthful breeze rustles into dances.
What is it you week for, pussy willow?

Mellow willow bats caressing leather
compliment your beauty.

Cricket's finest artists with willowy
elegance have charmed us for centuries.
None more so than David Gower, greying
golden curls abounding, as with showy
abandon he beguiled eager senses.
Sometime infuriating, insecure,
maybe we expected too much of his
sublime gifts. Willow patterns, not pretences
flowed from his mercurial, flashing blade.

Perhaps, pussy willow, you are weeping
for lost willow patterns.

∎

Daylight Saving
May Sumser

"Best part of the day,"
She said it was, the petrol-pump attendant,
"Best part of the day".

Summer Explosion

Sky clear. Wind gone away.
Hands of the clock crawled to the reckoning.
Spring was passing, beguiling, beckoning.
Petrol sang through the pipe,
A blackbird sang in the pinetree.
Rain had lashed the trees.
Late sunshine splashed the leaves.
Tank was filling.

I had letters to write,
Chores for the children:
A loveliness to lose.

Tank overflowed with power,
Petrol perfumed the air.
Petrol was the scent of apple-blossom,
Apple-blossom, pink and perfect.
Like a lamb the engine leapt.

"Just right, love," she said,
Taking the money.
"Going somewhere nice, are you?"

"To the apple-orchards," I said.

∎

Exam Time Again
Pat Jackson

A watch ticks on the desk
like a bomb.
Outside a skylark sings,
The sky is blue.

A shaft of sun
falls across the watch.
Through the open window
seeds of summer drift
and irritate the nose.

Summer Explosion

A plane scrawls in white,
 droning across blue.
In the distant green field
 poppies bleed.

Time blurs in front of runny eyes,
 pens scratch faster, legs fidget.
A bee bounces on the window pane
 desperate for summer meadows,
 brightly-coloured flowers.

A sneeze is fielded,
 clothes stick to the skin.
Somewhere a blackbird sings.
Examiner shouts "Time".

■

Summer Beach Day
Kaye Lee

The sea's rhythm
Of blue green white
Green blue green
White beats and sparkles,
The silver vibration
Advancing, retreating,
Pushing, pulling the gold
Of the crystalline shore.

The soft breeze, salted,
 Fingers my hair,
 Coolly explores

My heat-dewed angles.

High in the blue
Air seagulls squawk.
Two dripping, grinning,
 Lolloping dogs

Summer Explosion

leads hang
On the No Dogs Sign.

Movement and stillness,
Dark shadow, bright light,
The summer brown hills,
The cool, restless sea,
Similars and contrasts -
Balm for my frenzy.

■

Summer Days
Shirley Holmes

Childish squeals bring pleasure
to the coldest heart
as child-hood memories dance
on summer haze,
and golden sun kissed limbs
recline in soft oblivion.

Sunlight transforms the winter drab
into a honeyed taste of yester-year,
and happy souls succumb
to lazy days.

In full breasted trees
an abundance of sweet blossoms
snuggle in intimate contact,
warm gentle breezes stir
the senses as sunbeams
filter through reflections
glare...

■

Hard Sounds
Frank McGivern

Our strolling English lane in April,
Quiet but for birds,
Brings precious calm.
In May the first faint stirrings
As the hedges and their denizens burgeon.
No school holidays in June
So calm persists.

July roars into our lives!!
The cars and caravans appear,
Heading, lemmings, to the cliff.
All day, all night, they thunder through,
The lane their access to the sea.

Birdsong obliterated,
Leaves leaden with fume-filled dust;
Kids on picnic near the drive
Pissing while shouting,
In the privet.
Nothing any longer private:
Summer gone before it's truly started.

■

Bonnie Blackpool
Margaret C Rae

This is the centenary of Blackpool Tower
I feel I've been going there as long
With thousands of other people
Along the front we throng
They've painted the tower this year
Now the outside is really gold
Not just the beautiful ballroom
It stands out so proud and bold
Then there is the Pleasure Beach
So noisy, busy and brash

They have a new roller coaster
It takes you up and down in a flash
There is also the Sand Castle
If you like to play in a pool
With slides and waves in the water
It really is quite cool
With all the things there are to do
It doesn't matter if it rains
You'll always find somewhere to go
With Blackpool, who needs Spain?

∎

Meeting After Bad Light Stopped Play
Christine Ractliff

The wicket, on a desert sea of green,
Disappears in the dimness
Of an afternoon nightfall.
November in June.
The crowd in disappointment swells away,
You, the centre of a surge of silent faces.

But I am running, racing,
Faster than the humming train,
Thrumming heart outpacing
The wheels' drum-drumming on the track;
Jumping with a broom to brush away
The canopy of clouds;
Leaping to light the sun with matches -
To see the bright reflection in your eyes
Of summer joy.

∎

Summer Explosion

Ghosts Of Summer Past
Karen Crawcour

In the vast, sweet, green lawns
of Marble Hill House
a timeless tableau unfolds -
cool river breezes
brush the warm lips of lovers
who lay, in tender oblivion,
beneath the branches of ancient oaks;
dogs race, in uncontrolled exuberance,
in pursuit of omniscient black crows;
clusters of white-clad enthusiasts
perform a ballet of Eastern rituals;
and time-worn faces
wander slowly, in pairs,
along the winding paths.
Meanwhile, in the shadows
of the drooping willows,
and from behind the rich curtains,
of the House, spectres in rustling
silks and opulent taffetas
whisper desultory,
in the hazy heat,
eternally watching
the passing years.

∎

The Village Dog Show
Heather Smith

A bloodshot Bloodhound forced to trot
Seems unhappy with his lot;
Cavorting Corgis hop and skip
And sometimes have a sly old nip;
The rough-haired Lassie sort of collie
Seems quite clever and quite jolly;
Terrible terriers snarl and quiver
As if they might rip out a liver;

But soft-mouthed spaniels bounce and pant,
Appearing rather ignorant.
A pottering Pekinese just snuffles,
His features hidden in his ruffles;
While Mr. Afghan fairly flows
In his long and silken robes;
Alert Alsations follow closely,
Although, perhaps, a touch morosely.

But now the judging's almost done
- It seems the vicar's cat has won.

■

Berries
Jo Phillips

The raspberries that you froze
were thawed this morning,
ice melting to drops
on each segment.

It was hot among the canes
as we picked together
tented in netting
screened in green.

And you didn't see me
as I slipped away
but I heard you talking
to me not there.

What were you saying
that last short summer?
Why didn't I listen
to you still here?

■

Summer Explosion

Thoughts On Summer
Eileen Kyte

When I think of summer
I think of many things
Like milk turning sour
And butter melting
No rain for days
Hose pipes are banned
To water the garden I go
Bucket in hand

Queuing for half an hour for an ice-cream
Only to see it melt before my tea
But still the gardens look so pretty
When at last summer do arrive
It's amazing how the plants and seeds survived
The cold winds frost and snow
And now at last they have grown

Roses wallflowers and geraniums too
are just to name a few
All different colours shapes and sizes
They make the garden look alive
All standing in rows and rows
They make quite a colourful show

Then going to the local fete
I can hardly wait
To try my hand at throwing things
Hoping something I will win

■

Summer Show
Pam Gidney

The garden celebrates summer
With an explosion of light and colour,
Like Firework Night without the bangs.

Summer Explosion

Enormous Catherine Wheels of sunflowers
Rotate towards the sun;
Rockets of red-hot pokers seem to be waiting
For someone to light the blue touch-paper;
The seeds of Busy Lizzies are shooting everywhere
Like squibs, at the touch of a finger.
Golden rod spills yellow flares of light,
While lupins hold their coloured spikes aloft
Like stately Roman candles,
And the laburnum tree, ablaze with gold,
Flings its cascading blossom against the blue
Like rocket-bursts which lighten the night sky
In cold November. People come to gaze,
Mesmerised by the excitement of it all.
Children hold aloft the dandelion-puffs
Like sparklers, waving them about
Till they are quite extinguished.

So all these firework-flowers
Scatter their seeds to make the future sure;
And though November's bonfires burn their husks
They will renew themselves when summer comes
And once again put on their dazzling show.

■

Summer
Robert P Reed

The pebbles crunched underfoot...
By the waters edge
We collected seashells,
Ancient and worn.

The windsurfers sails flitted to and fro
Beneath the deep blue sky;
Like brightly coloured butterflies
Skimming the waves.

113

Summer Explosion

Happily, I watched you laugh and scream,
As the surf rolled in,
An oceanic heartbeat
Breaking against your legs;
The foam caressing your thighs.

I remember the taste
Of the salt on your lips
And the aroma of the sea
In your dark hair...

■

Cloud Racing
Pamela Reed

Sapphires' seeping across the air.
Banishing; the grey rains' lair,
As quiet cumulus cloud races past,
Casting dark shadow on jade grass,
The cloud chariot galloping still.
He suddenly turns; feline at will
Stalking across the brilliant sky
As giant mouse comes creeping by.

■

Summer Senses
Felicity Minifie

Squabbling starlings.
Children's merry shouting.
Happy splashes in the sea.
Noisy machines on a Sunday morn.
Trimming hedges and mowing the lawn.

Cucumber sandwiches.
Strawberries with cream.
Out in the garden for tea.
Salty spray as we jumped over waves.
Warm beer, greasy chips at all-night raves.

Summer Explosion

I go back to the days.
When I was so young.
Sun-kissed limbs. short-trousered knee.
Sizzling sausages on the flames.
Smutty smells of the holiday trains.

Drops of sweat stream down.
Red sun-flushed faces.
Cold waves shocked bare sandy me.
Gritty food we pretend to enjoy.
Buckets and spades, the favourite toy.

That golden orb shines.
A dazzling blue sky.
Flower, butterfly and bee.
Dance in the warmth, praising joyfully.
Summer's bounteous abundancy.

■

Summer Symphony
Kathleen Gillum

To wake up on a summer morn
And greet the day at crack of dawn,
And gaze in wonder at the world,
Upon green grass with dew impearled.
The earth seems washed and clean and bright
In rays of opalescent light.
Old scenes are viewed with fresh new eyes
As sunshine streams from summer skies.

And birdsong from each hedge and tree
Combines in perfect harmony
To lift the heart, and spirit raise,
From feathered throats comes notes of praise.
And flowers in their leafy dress
Stand out in vibrant vividness,
In colours vital, striking, bold,
Yellow and crimson, blue and gold.

Summer Explosion

A dragonfly is on the go
With darting movements to and fro,
Neon body, shimmering wings,
One amongst many special things
Observed by us this time of year,
No need to doubt that summer's here.
I'm awed at the variety
In Nature's summer symphony.

∎

Maytime In Cuerden
Diane Parkin

The park was bathed in beauty and in the summer sun
the trees were stretched in languor,
the world was having fun
On the day the cranes came to Cuerden.

The diggers struck the first shock before the clock struck nine
contractors culling countryside
so the suits could be on time
On the day the cranes came to Cuerden.

The nest was naked, open, broken eggshells pale and dun
the tree ripped from its mother earth
only fifty years young
On the day the cranes came to Cuerden.

The protesters' voices rang clear across the dell
but they can't compete with Westminster
tolling the knell
On the day the cranes came to Cuerden.

The devastation far outstripped that of the wire or the gun
and set the shattered ground to moaning
for the animals yet to come
On the day the cranes came to Cuerden.

Summer Explosion

Love At First Sight
Mollie Bolt

This is a city made for summer;
Not meant to be remembered in the rain.
Chestnuts and copper beeches on a residential hill,
Buildings still beautiful
After two hundred years. The streets speak history...
Time's finger beckons, and the past appears.

Legions were here, amid the Mendips re-creating Rome;
But finding England: some, at least,
May well have ceased to dream of home.

In Bath, the bridges shimmer in the sun;
And one must drift, and lean, and gaze.
The longest days are short of hours
Too weary of its scenes.

To linger here means never to be free:
Remembering England now, I think I see
Crescents and terraces, through tears, as lovers do;
I have been spellbound by a summer city:
It has enchanted me, and torn my heart in two.

∎

Rondo
James Dixon

What shall we do with the old third movement?
Who cares, we haven't much left to prove ent
er early to drown out any comment,
Just to keep them guessing.

How can you follow the lovely slow part
But downhill from a pretty low start?
How should we know when it baffled Mozart?
Please let's skip the repeat.

Summer Explosion

Play very fast and don't look up much,
You might see the lady in the fifth row back touch
Her husband's sleeve cos she forgot her watch,
Yes we've lost their interest.

It's hot and late and value's been had,
What's left when you've used up happy and sad?
Two-and-a-half out of three ain't so bad,
Just time for a trick ending.

Ending,
Ending,
Ending,
Ending,

End,

End,

End,

Ha!
Caught you out!

■

Midsummer Memory
Margaret Lawson

Midsummer Morning - and up with the lark.
(Fragrant the kitchen with baking)
Midsummer Music - the birdsong, oh hark!
(Scones and new rolls are a-making.)
Look at the sky, such a radiant blue.
See how the sunlight is dancing.
"Just the right morning - I think so, don't you?
The woods will be simply entrancing."

Look at the sky, how it steadily pours!
See how the branches are dripping.

Sandwiches soaking and nowhere to sit:
Though hot is the tea we are sipping.
Midsummer Misery - still only noon?
(So dismal to be a poor vagrant)
Midsummer Madness - a picnic in June.
(And oh! for that kitchen so fragrant!)

■

Summer Journey
Lorna Grinter

Light splices through verdant leaves,
Wind scythes the common
Wrestling with sights and sounds.
On this day, bright with greenness,
I am ready,
Stretched by five long summers,
To tread in his October footprints.

His marks made permanent
By the soft breathing
Of forgotten winds.
His words still wispy fragments
In the calm air.

I tread my journey
Through squirrel pathways,
Through blossom and bramble,
Until I find them -
his prints.

I lie immersed in dried mud
and half remembered promises.

■

Summer Explosion

Late Summer Evening
Elise Hawker

The garden has a generous hilly top
enclosing a lazy spinney
hiding plaintive wood-pigeons

Bracken-haired slopes across the valley
knowingly reflect the evening light
yet cover rabbits in abandoned play

Somewhere down in the village a dog barks
and birds chatter in mixed octaves
but quiet gains the hold of twilit day

The sounds there are, accentuate the peace
so that a distant train becomes deep harmony
sheep in the high fields, accented phrases

Each tree and shrub was planted here with love
designed, but now under nature's acceptance
thrusting upward and out, receiving butterflies

From all angles the house is seen
peeping from it's white-paint windows
under watchful eyebrows of mellowed tiles

Soon, shadows will deepen the greens
squirrels begin their early hoard of summer stores
warily listening to the small breeze

Evening is kind along this valley
slowly covers and encloses all things
into a cavern of slumber

■

Summer Explosion

Strawberry Flair
Elsie D Gee

Furrows of strawberries, mantled in straw,
Happy families pick punnets galore.
Children with fingers and lips stained red,
Mothers in sunhats, "No more, I've said".
Everyone quietly picking in rows,
Thinking of strawberry jam on scones,
Pavlovas, trifles, strawberries with cream,
All of these pictures colour my dream.
And when I return it's on with the pan:
After washing and draining hard work then began;
Stirring and stirring hot cauldrons of jam,
I'll remember this day as long as I can.

■

Summer In The Pyrenees
Sheila M Churchill

Summer heat melts winter snow, on Pyrenian pinnacles
Jagged crests of crystal spikes thrust upwards to the azure sky
As Nature's loving dance in May invites the touching of the sun

Biting chill, with soft persuasion, yields itself to pillowed warmth
Sunlit fingers, amber toasted, play their music on the spurs
To free the captive mountain meadows from a frozen dark embrace

Ice converts to boisterous cascades, arching, etching down the gorge
Bursting fresh in summer sunshine on the dormant austere earth
To romp with fledgling daisy rings upon the grassy slopes below

Summer Explosion

Armchair hollow, snow impacted, slump and slip to join the flow
Dappled rays, in concentration, thaw the glacier in its path
And rapids plunge, in wild abandon, merging with the waterfalls

Pine and aspen, rooted firmly, line the ridges sheer and sharp
Lichen clings to scattered boulders in the milk white foaming streams
As joyful new-born rivers start their journeys to the distant sea

Alpine flowers lift their blossoms, stretching petals to the sun
Bravely cleaving to the rockface, nurtured by the balmy air
For life erupts around them now, to live before the summer dies

Fragrant pastures beckon welcome, coaxing butterflies to rest
Limpid pools of pure spring water mirror intertwining ferns
As hovering wings of searching bees court bending buds of columbine

Radiant summer in Gavarnie, high amidst the Pyrenees,
Striding hikers roam its valley, donkeys clop along its paths
This domain of grace and beauty keeps the promise of rebirth

∎

Summer's Lease
Roxane Houston

Step out into the sun! There is no time
To waste,
No time to hesitate!
Your life is to be lived, not set aside
To ponder on.

Summer Explosion

Step out into the sun! Whom will you blame
If joy
Is soured that comes too late,
And love remains mere mystery beside
To wonder at?

How long will summer wait? For it must wax
And wane
As it has always done.
Unlatch your shuttered heart! Here is a world
To wander in!
How long will summer wait? You cannot coax
A day
Beyond its legal span.
And what is left if life itself grows cold,
And love remains mere mystery
To wonder at?

■

Wish You Were Here
Dora Stubbs

As through the sand we kids all trudges our feet began to
sink
'cause after all we had the lot except the kitchen sink
With Mum's transistor, all the deckchairs, sarnies by the
core
talk about the camel's back we couldn't carry more.
Old granddad with his hanky, corners knotted on his head
Watched our old man give orders as he laid out on a bed
Then Willie bawled his head off and created lots of hassle
Just because a blooming dog ran through his flaming castle
Dad struggled back with ice-creams nearly melted in the
sun
Got 'em nearly handed round except the strawberry one
That slithered gently from its cone just like some pink
Houdini
and settled neatly down inside the front of Mum's bikini.
Well Gran turned from her paddling to catch up with the
joking

Summer Explosion

Didn't see the tide come in and got her knickers soaking.
Eventually things settled down, in fact became quite boring
Gran sat doing crosswords and Mum and Dad were snoring.
Then Granddad took a hand in things and called us to his side
"Come on you kids, we'll have some fun, we'll have a donkey ride".
And then we lost our Maureen and all went looking for her
Found her reading donkey's names, had picked the one called Dora.
The first one was right stubborn and we all got stuck behind her,
Dug her hooves in, stood her ground and dropped a small reminder.
Oh happy days that one for sure stands in my memory
That day began the love affair between me and the sea

■

Surreal Summer
Gillian Tindall

Flowers! Dewy-coloured remnants of my kaleidoscope memory
Of scents and grassy, luscious smells.

I tasted juicy brambles and drank rain from the leafy cups
Of papery poppy shells; and never wished for paradise in the hells
Of interloping fears and black cavernous dreams,
My waking sleep was entwined with ivy green, clinging
To my wet throat, a weeping tree with the sap pouring out.

My ears were not stuffed with the peat clod, although my nostrils'
Hairs caressed the earthy smell. I heard nature's music and recognised
Its tune well: it was the song of psalms which every bird sings
As horizon sun mounts the clouds, and rocks powerfully to and fro

Summer Explosion

On the sky's azure back until the heat of its list is sated.

It is true that time flies with the crickets: they have clicking
Ticking clocks on wings.
Blue bottled twist to escape an unknown fate,
Choosing the helter skelter way, looping loops and climbing
cloudways to the skies.
While down below them, hanging in the hazy air,
fat-groomed bumble bees
float on solidifying sound; upheld by nothing but their tiny
grandeur.

They all protest until succumbing sun relents
And the ease of evening trickles from the streamlet's mossy
grove,
Where wild hyacinths - purple carpeted dream - force the
skies
Down to earth level.

∎

Sunset Over Mull
David Oliver

Summer evening on the Sound of Mull
distillation of peace
modulating tangerine sky
gentle scouring of the tie
slapping slurping
rhythmical barnacles hollows
tiny boat leaves Tobermory
tracing a golden shimmer

Silent minutes of propagation
waves of harmonic calm
scattering bejewelled surface
stranded purple jellyfish
vibrating desiccating
black tendrils of elastic weed
green ribbons heat-welded to rock
quivering in mirror pool

Summer Explosion

Mull's mountains rotate towards the sun
Ben More's pyramid face
glows peach in the conflagration
lower hills discarding lines
shading fading
darkness fast engulfing the scene
beware treacherous pathway home
above the blackening Sound

■

INDEX

A Brand New Day	*51*
A Child's Delight	*29*
A Day To Love	*33*
A Garden	*32*
A Lovely Day	*40*
A Midsummer Daydream	*66*
A Scene Between Two Trees	*99*
A Summers Day	*2*
After The Fire	*95*
Alfresco	*59*
An English Country Garden	*5*
An Ode To Paul	*22*
Artificial Roses	*47*
At The Red Deer	*25*
August Holidays	*30*
Bank Holiday Monday	*58*
Beach Party	*66*
Beauty	*34*
Berries	*111*
Blackbird	*17*
Blessings	*72*
Bonnie Blackpool	*108*
Booming Summer	*18*
Bright Days	*4*
Burning Strawberry June	*89*
Butterflies	*86*
Catamaran - Regatta Bound	*65*
Childhood Memories	*94*
Cloud Racing	*114*
Crowned In Glory	*101*
Dark Tunnel	*53*
Day Return	*14*
Daylight Saving	*104*
Double Summertime	*55*
Even To The Dust	*28*
Evocation	*23*
Exam Time Again	*105*
Fertility	*52*

Summer Explosion

Ghosts Of Summer Past	110
Goodbye Summer	63
Happy Romance	49
Hard Sounds	108
Harmony	56
Headmistress's Duty	41
Holiday Fortnight At Home	61
How Can We Help The Policeman?	43
I Remember	75
I Walked In The Country	37
In Abingdon Abbey Garden	36
In Eternity's Sunrise	93
It's A Car's Life	8
Jewels In The Aegean Sea	20
Joys Of Summer	47
Laburnums	11
Late Summer Evening	120
Life	84
Life's Summer	9
Loneliness	90
Louise	42
Love At First Sight	117
Love, Light And Warmth	64
Maypole Dance 1959	71
Maytime In Cuerden	116
Meeting After Bad Light Stopped Play	109
Memories	20
Memories	85
Memories Of A Lover	52
Midsummer Lane	83
Midsummer Memory	118
Monstrosity Of Nature	43
Moon	87
My Cappuccino Love	77
My Seasons	27
Nasturtiums	100
Nature's Trail	56
Nellie's Only Outing	19
New Forest In Summer	2
Oh Lucky Me	48
Old English Summer	31

Summer Explosion

On The River	*45*
One Afternoon	*69*
Only Just Sunbathing	*63*
Our Family Motto!	*87*
Outhouse Overture	*39*
Paradox '94	*9*
Portrait Of Village Life	*68*
Prairie Sunrise	*97*
Rainbow (Rondeau)	*10*
Raspberry Ripple	*96*
Riding	*39*
Rondo	*117*
Rose Garden	*1*
Sings - Now The Summer	*26*
Sonething I Said?	*46*
Strawberry Flair	*121*
Summary	*12*
Summer	*49*
Summer	*113*
Summer	*59*
Summer Beach Day	*106*
Summer Bliss	*82*
Summer By The Sea	*78*
Summer Days	*41*
Summer Days	*107*
Summer Explosion	*100*
Summer Fever	*91*
Summer Flirt	*35*
Summer In Andorra	*96*
Summer In The Pyrenees	*121*
Summer Is Coming	*74*
Summer Is To Me	*77*
Summer Journey	*119*
Summer Madness	*1*
Summer Magic	*72*
Summer Senses	*114*
Summer Show	*112*
Summer Sun	*98*
Summer Symphony	*115*
Summer Time	*6*
Summer's Explosion	*37*

Summer Explosion

Summer's Inspiration	5
Summer's Lease	122
Summer's Song	38
Summerland	80
Summertime	25
Sun Day	18
Sunburn	16
Sunday Menu	7
Sunset Over Mull	125
Sunshine In The Rain	81
Surreal Summer	124
Tableau	21
Tanfalier	60
The Beachcomber	57
The Black Flower	51
The Dainty Blue Butterfly	65
The Day Tripper	70
The Dream	93
The Empire Hotel, Blackpool	10
The Environment	86
The Gift Of Summer	15
The Golden Burst	103
The Gymkhana	13
The Human Race	44
The Jewel	76
The Jumble Sale	92
The Season's Symphony	15
The Seasons Of Love	45
The Shore On Longboat Key, Florida	32
The Single State	27
The Stream	84
The Summer Morning	90
The Time Between	73
The Urban Princess And The Peony	102
The View From The Hill	16
The Village Dog Show	110
The Year Abroad	67
Thoughts Of England	50
Thoughts On Summer	112
To A Butterfly Found Dead	24
Twilight	62

Summer Explosion

Unborn Child	*82*
United Beach Mission	*29*
Valley Of Song	*102*
Welcome To Summer	*12*
Welcome Visitors	*79*
What Is A Summer's Day?	*34*
Where, Oh Where Is The Summer?	*88*
Who's Got Sunburn	*61*
Whortleberry Pie	*54*
Willow Patterns	*104*
Wish You Were Here	*123*
Wishes Upon A Warm Day	*62*
You Fresh Optimistic Thing	*76*
Youthful Summer	*3*